"In this thoughtful book, Katie se[…]
tractions, *calls* us to something de[…]
remembering Him, and *engages* us w[…]
take us into a far richer knowledge oɪ ɪɪɪs ɪaɪtɪɪuɪɪness.

> Susan Alexander Yates, speaker and bestselling author of *Risky Faith: Becoming Brave Enough to Trust the God Who Is Bigger than Your World* and *The One Devotional*

"'Do not forget,' wrote Moses, David, other psalmists, Solomon, the prophets. Remembering matters to our God. Now, a new voice for a new generation, Katie Westenberg, is exhorting us to remember. We need this challenge. Read her book and take her words to heart!"

> Barbara Rainey, wife, mom, and mimi; author, artist, and seminary student; founder of EverThineHome.com

"Katie gently reminds us that with every click and scroll, we are disciplining our minds toward inattention to the things that matter most. *But Then She Remembered* calls us to consider the true cost of our distraction and encourages us to rededicate ourselves to loving God with our whole minds."

> Sarah Beals, author of Joyfilleddays.com and writer/contributor at Club31Women

"In an age with endless distractions and jam-packed schedules, when memory tends to be delegated to our phones, it's easy to get sidetracked, settling into voluntary amnesia. *But Then She Remembered* reminds us of the richness found in remembering and gently guides us in renewing this God-ordained pursuit."

> Heather Haupt, author of *Knights in Training: Ten Principles for Raising Honorable, Courageous, and Compassionate Boys*

"This book is for anyone who has walked into a room and forgotten what she came for. It's also for anyone who has walked into a crisis and forgotten God. This book is good. Really good.

In fact, the only bad thing with *But Then She Remembered* is that you will want to remember it—every chapter, every word—and you won't be able to. You will (happily) have to read it again. And again. And . . ."

Jodie Berndt, author and speaker

but then
she
remembered

but then she remembered

how to give God your *full attention*
in a distracted world

Katie Westenberg

BETHANYHOUSE

a division of Baker Publishing Group
Minneapolis, Minnesota

Published by Bethany House Publishers
Minneapolis, Minnesota
www.bethanyhouse.com

Bethany House Publishers is a division of
Baker Publishing Group, Grand Rapids, Michigan

Printed in the United States of America

ISBN 978-0-7642-3542-9 (paper)
ISBN 978-1-4934-4073-3 (ebook)
ISBN 978-0-7642-4161-1 (casebound)

Library of Congress Control Number: 2022053714

Cover design by Studio Gearbox

Author represented by D.C. Jacobson & Associates LLC

Baker Publishing Group publications use paper produced from sustainable forestry practices and post-consumer waste whenever possible.

23 24 25 26 27 28 29   7 6 5 4 3 2 1

To my grandmother, stalwart in her swishy skirt and bright lipstick in that Sunday morning pew.

And the other, who sang vibrantly, fully off key and yet fully given. To my grandfather who finally found faith and was baptized long after his hair was white.

And the other, who met Jesus on his deathbed.

Your faith and faithfulness have been my inheritance. With David, I give profound thanks; the Lord has given me a heritage of those who fear His name. These words, and the whole of my life, have been hemmed by it.

Thank you.

contents

A Note for the Distracted   11

1. The World Has Lost Its Memory   17

2. Beginning with What We Must Know   33

3. Actions that Bring Us Back to Remembrance   55

4. Who You Are and How You Were Made   77

5. God's View of Time, Not Ours   97

6. Say So—*Why telling the story matters*   117

7. Remembering When You Feel Weak   135

8. Habit forming—*Training to become rememberers*   155

Afterword   179
Acknowledgments   181
Notes   183
About the Author   191

a note for the
distracted

I stood in the trailing self-checkout line at Target the day after Christmas, happy to purchase my two three-dollar decorative Christmas trees—70 percent off, friend, a steal—and a young mama who looked as though she may have walked straight out of the oft-recycled meme about moms and Target runs stood just behind me. You've seen those memes, right? A mom with a tiny tot tucked carefully in her heaping cart of Christmas clearance items. "Mama." Her little girl's sweetly shrill voice invited the attention of shoppers within no small radius. "I think we got . . . *distracted*." "Yes." The mama took the pint-sized admonition in stride as she surveyed the overwhelming contents of her shopping cart. "We got very, *very* distracted."

I smiled back at the mother-daughter pair. They were cute. Stereotypical. But the eavesdropped conversation brought to mind a greater question I had been wrestling with for a few years already—at what point is our distraction . . . *not cute*? We make jokes about our lack of focus, our lack of intention and attention, on the regular. To the point, apparently, that even our toddlers know the gig. Perhaps the pace of our lives and our distracted state have become so familiar, so commonplace, so normal, that we hardly even notice what is lost. But it is worth considering— what is the real risk of a distracted life?

I have no war to wage with that Target mama because I have been her. At times I still am her, although the terms and conditions vary. I've long run out of toddlers to tote around, but the temptation toward distraction seems quite comfortable to age with me. I can wake early to make space to pause, flip open my Bible, to seek and to knock, only to find my brain is not inclined to follow suit. Even when my body slows, my mind is too often loath to respond in kind. It races or drifts without permission, firing off notifications—the text I didn't respond to, the wrinkled laundry that I will need to tumble through the drier one more time, the world news that seems to be a continual weight, and that phone call I keep failing to make for the appointment I don't really want to have. *What is the weather going to be like today, anyway?* A barrage of thoughts present themselves with a newfound urgency when I try to pause, focus. I forget them with fervor, honestly, until I actually want to remember. And then it all feels important.

I'm so distracted.

You're here, friend, so I know you feel it too. But my concern is for far more than just our feelings. My concern is for the greater costs of living a distracted life. What do we stand to lose in a life of whiplashed attention, incubated in an attention economy, where our gaze, our minutes, our thoughts and actions, are the currency the world around us is trading in? Why does the world we live in seem to value our attention more than we do? We know our days are numbered. We know Christ's return is imminent. So what do we stand to lose when we give way to a distracted life? I believe the stakes are high, friend, so I'll give them to you straight.

- **Relationship with Christ** because He said He would make His home with us,[1] and often we're just too busy scrolling, too focused on that to-do list, to even engage with Him.
- **Trust in God** because we're quick to forget His faithfulness in the past and remember He will be faithful in every tomorrow.
- **Connection with others** because we have at least fifteen tabs open in our brains even on a quiet day. We're barely cognizant of all the missed connections.
- **The ability to focus on our work** because we are weighed down with worry of every sort.
- **Rest** because our brains continue to buzz even when our bodies beg for sleep.
- **Peace** because our minds and bodies groan under the stress and strain of constant urgency and we're quick to forget where to find help.
- **Embracing God's grandeur right in front of us**—the beauty in our homes, the extravagance of creation, and the richness of relationship are gifts we miss when we aren't really "here" because our minds are somewhere else.
- **Perspective** because our emotions roll along with the latest news cycle. We feel desperate—or even worse, numb—when we aren't presently anchored by the truth of eternity.
- **Our heritage.** We're living one and leaving one—the substance of which will be precisely the sum of what we have spent our days chasing after.

The stakes are indeed high.

In its simplest form, distraction is a drawing or dragging away from that which we intend to focus on. Its impact often feels slight, barely noticeable, hardly a problem, but it encroaches beyond the current moment. Distraction becomes a conditioning, a training of sorts. Our eyes, our minds, and ultimately our hearts, become increasingly fitted and shaped for the drawing away. Distraction is a steady tide pounding the surf and over time, reshaping the shore, reshaping us. In distraction, we concede direction. And like the shore shaping tide, it all happens very gradually.

A recent study of a thousand cell phone users in the U.S. revealed that 47 percent consider themselves addicted to their cell phone.[2] Nearly half! We could call the details and parameters of this survey into question. We could argue the definitions and question the terms, but at a most basic level, do you know what this survey tells us? This survey tells us that we aren't naïve. We are not ignorant to the pull to check in or scroll, to refresh the feed or comment, to feel connected or liked or seen. We are not completely unaware of the drawing and dragging away, the hours that are whiled away, but the battle is still likely far greater than we recognize.

What if the physical effects of distraction are only symptomatic of a more important issue in the life of the believer? What if eyes prone to wonder become correlative to a heart that is much the same? What if a mind fueled by pinball patterns of thinking, emaciated from the kind of focus that could provide any real sustenance, becomes a mind that struggles to linger with the Lord, to remember His ways, who He is, and how He loves? What if distraction is far more dangerous than we realize, and by our very design, we were made for so much more?

I've done it just like you have, friend. I've mixed up my kids' names, forgotten what I've walked into a room for, and failed to remember the simple things that matter most in a whirl of my own lack of focus. I have ignored and neglected and been irked by distractions, but I have come to learn that these frustrations are worth noting. External distraction often gives way to internal distraction, and it is vital that we lead our hearts with wisdom here. We are charged in God's Word to take every thought captive, but we live in a world that invites us to follow every rabbit trail of thought (and belief) possible. It's all easily accessible via the swipe of your finger, the vibration on your wrist. We navigate our lives on devices that vie insatiably for our attention and continually orient our thoughts toward the immediate and the urgent over the eternal. They craftily play to our weakest vulnerabilities—a fear of disconnection, of missing out, of being unseen. But the greater risk is the reshaping of our souls to mere fragments of their original design—hearts that long to be found in relationship with our Creator, loving Him with all our heart and soul, mind and strength.

Our attempts at reform have been less than helpful. We're still here, drowning in distraction that is warring in our souls. But we know, we must remember, though we walk in the flesh, we do not wage war in the flesh.[3] We are empowered to stand firm in the strength and might of the Lord, alert with all perseverance when we take up the armor Christ has offered to us, rather than the wisdom of this present age.[4] We don't need to manage symptoms; we need to unpack the timeless truth of God's Word to speak to our current predicament. The One who created and designed our very minds also created us for obedience here. He designed us for perseverance and endurance. He has fitted us for it, called us to it, and it is time we began to employ the wisdom of the Designer, in the battle to love Him with our minds. This is a fight for focus—a call to lay aside the hindrance so easily ensnaring our minds and our hearts, that we might walk in a manner worthy of our calling. It is time that we remember, friend.

The stakes are high because we are made for more. As believers, we are made to abide in Christ and bear fruit,[5] but far too many of us are plagued with a cancer that just won't quit growing. I believe distraction is causing us to unknowingly quench the Spirit, the very Helper who works to grow that good fruit in us.

Patience is His fruit in us. Joy and peace are the fruit He grows in us. The love we are so desperately trying to drum up for the broken world around us—the kind of love that the Father has for His own Son—is a fruit of His Spirit that has been given to us. I don't know about you, but I want more of that. I don't want to leave that on the table, forgetting what has been afforded to me at no small cost.

I fear we're missing out, friend, and it's not the FOMO we have become accustomed to. We have forgotten what it's like to know God and *remember* Him. In the noise and distraction of this world, we have forgotten what He has promised and how that truth transforms. It not only changes our future, but our day, our minutes and moments, our now. We live in a world that needs to hear and know and see truth on display through virtue—real life lived out by women who know how to pay attention to what matters most. We have the opportunity to be purveyors of that truth in our homes, in our communities, and for the next generation. We have an incredibly high calling. It is time we got serious about paying attention. It is time we got better at remembering. You ready, friend? Let's go.

1

the world has lost
its memory

I sat across the table from Ross at Panera. We were on a stolen date of sorts, the unplanned, last-minute, squished-in-between-all-the-things kind. Squished-in-between lunches can, by God's grace, sustain a marriage quite well in a busier season of life with four active kids.

He had the pepperoni pizza—flatbread for the purists, but I assure you, its pepperoni pizza for Ross. By contrast, I had a warm Mediterranean bowl with chicken. This might be the simplest way I could introduce you to us. Two decades ago, we got into a legitimate argument over pizza toppings, but we're twenty years in and we have this (mostly) figured out now. We don't share pizza. We run parallel on the things that matter, and freely, gladly dissent on food choice.

But that rarely stops me from trying to convince Ross that my more unique food preferences are really where it's at. "You've gotta try this!" I tell him. "Quinoa and feta. Grape tomatoes and chopped cucumber. Some sort of tzatziki and . . . and . . ." I fumbled for a familiar word that was somehow just out of mind's reach. "The, uh . . . this. Why can't I think of the word?" Ross wasn't tracking with me. "I have no idea what you're talking about," he declared bluntly.

I have little patience with my mind when it plays sluggish games. I tried to get Ross to help me. "Yes you do. It's mashed up chickpeas. We dip carrots and celery in it (at least I do). Why can't I think of that silly word?" The light bulb comes on for Ross. "Oh yeah, I know what you're talking about! But I don't remember what it's called either." And now I'm officially annoyed. How can two capable adults, who have each managed to navigate more than four decades of life and keep four kids mostly thriving, fail to remember the name of the chickpea condiment in my warm Mediterranean bowl. I remembered the name of tzatziki, for goodness' sake. And we know quinoa—I ruined it for Ross a few years back by serving tabbouleh too frequently. *Tzatziki* and *tabbouleh* aren't everyday words for us, yet we remembered them without pause. But the moniker for chickpea paste? It vanished.

I reached for my phone to end this silliness, but Ross stopped me short. "Don't do it," he urged. "Don't Google it. That's lazy. Force your brain to do the work." It's a little bit humbling to be a writer, a woman who literally works in the economy of words, and yet be so easily stumped. It's even more humbling to be writing a book on remembrance and trip over your own forgetfulness in elementary fashion during lunch at Panera. And then to have your husband tell you to *make your brain do the work*? God knew I would need this kind of man.

So rather than be annoyed, we unofficially played a game. I did surveillance around the word, unpacking everything I knew about it, and we would somehow figure it out. *I buy it at Costco and it comes with a little roasted red pepper sauce on top and a few pine nuts. But I've also bought the single-serving packs on occasion. But* . . . nothing. The name still evaded us. I imagined the packaging, the maroon label with matching lid, the lettering and font. Maybe I could *see* the word? Nope. Nothing. *People put it on pita. It's simple to make, add garlic and olive oil. I love it with cucumbers.* Still nothing. I so badly wanted to Google, to phone a friend at the least, but I knew Ross was right. If I want my mental muscles to work, then I need to make them work.

As it goes, the word came out a minute or two later, shortly after we stopped looking so hard for it. *"Hummus!"* I said a tad too loud. The word itself wasn't all that satisfying. I may have been holding a grudge against it. Really, if I'm going to forget a word, let's make it something a little more difficult, a little more impressive. But hummus? Yep, hummus.

But you know what was satisfying? The mental effort. It is good to be reminded of the limitations of my human brain as well as the beauty of God's created design to help me recall and think and *remember*. He created us to remember.

Why begin a book with a light story of common forgetfulness? Because I think you can relate. We live in a fast-paced world with a staggering number of distractions, and it is a real struggle to force our brains to focus anymore. It's hard to remember. We mostly learn to put up with the forgetfulness, fortifying ourselves with some quick fixes. I see you, Google, lowering the standard on what we deem to be an acceptable level of distraction. We throw around excuses like "It's just Mommy brain" or "pandemic fog," and while those may be legit, I'm beginning to wonder if they come with an expiration date. Is this just our new normal?

But that's not really the point. The point is that distraction and forgetfulness are trending. We have bloated calendars that make us anxious, and fifteen tabs open in our brains. We are multitasking our multitasking, and it's all laced with legitimate worries of the day, of the world, that feel paralyzing. That's real. We live in a world that is so loud, so opinionated, that it is not only exhausting, but immobilizing, and we have no idea how to fix it. So we scroll.

There is something far greater at risk here. Distracted eyes are leading to distracted souls. I can forget the word *hummus* for the rest of my life with little ill effect, but when distraction and forgetfulness leech into my soul, I have a far greater issue. Do you see it, friend?

I'm pretty sure mamas have been misfiring their own kids' names for as long as women have been having children, but what happens when the distractions creep further, wider, deeper? What happens when so-called normal forgetfulness inches toward something far more problematic—when in distraction we are tempted to forget what we are called for, called to? What happens when we forget truth? Our muscles of attention, our actual ability to rightly *attend to* something and do the work of remembering, are beginning to atrophy in a world of easy work-arounds and fillers. We reflexively reach for a quick fix or a surface solution, but I believe it's time we begin strengthening these muscles and addressing the root issue. We are quickly becoming a generation of fast forgetters. We are being trained to opt for the immediate at the risk of the important, a bait and switch we barely notice. In conceding eyes that fight for focus and resist distraction, we concede a heart and mind that follow suit. The cost is greater than we realize.

Time to Stretch

According to some hotly debated research from Microsoft, attention spans have plummeted to embarrassing levels.[1] I'm guessing you aren't surprised. We know this, but peeking at the research is akin to stepping on the scales. We look away, ignore the evidence. In the year 2000, experts estimated that the average attention span of adults was around twelve seconds. Yes, seconds. By 2013, that average dwindled to a mere eight seconds. *Are you still with me?* The stats are not in your favor. Or mine.

The kicker? Well, it's twofold. First, to give a little perspective, the report also claimed that goldfish have an average attention span of nine seconds. Remember, we're bottoming out at eight . . . so, that is something. But also, in case you'd didn't notice, 2013 was a decade ago. We lost four seconds—a quarter of our attention span—in the thirteen short years between the two surveys. Anyone else feel uncomfortable about where we are likely at today?

It is interesting that in a world of plummeting attention spans, much of the language of attention seems to have been relegated to antiquity as well. No doubt words follow trends and fall out of fashion, but in the process, we sometimes concede clarity. We sometimes concede truth. The word *attention* comes from the Latin *attendere*, which literally means "to stretch toward." Imagine that—like the zinnia starts in my windowsill right now, daily stretching up and out, directing their stems toward the sunlight by means of a natural process called phototropism. Or the way you incline yourself, leaning in toward a friend in conversation in a crowded and noisy room. We know what it looks like to stretch toward.

From *attendere* we derive the English verb "to attend," which now commonly means "to be present at." You attend a school board meeting, attend church, attend a wedding—all of which imply little more than the fact that you were there. No stretching needed. But centuries ago, the word came with far more of its original meaning. To attend to something was not merely to be present in body, but to be fully engaged toward it. To attend was to regard with attention.[2]

Along with *attend* came such verbs as *hearken*, which means "to attend to what is uttered with eagerness or curiosity,"[3] and *heed*, which means "to mind, to regard with care and attend to."[4] And of course *attention*, which according to Webster's 1828 Dictionary, meant the very act of attending or heeding. Today's definition, according to Webster, is "the act or state of applying the mind to something."[5] It's not difficult to see that we've lost something in trends and translation. We've robbed the word of its care and regard, of its eagerness and curiosity. We've forsaken the stretching toward and now find it sufficiently encompassing to simply apply our mind toward things. At least for a solid eight seconds.

In his book *The Rise and Triumph of the Modern Self*, Carl Trueman addresses our temptation to yearn for a lost golden age of the past when pitted against the superficiality of the present. He states, "The task of the Christian is not to whine about the moment in which he or she lives, but to understand its problems and respond appropriately to them."[6] If the modern problem here is the malnourishment of our existing language, considering Trueman's exhortation, I will refrain from bemoaning the richness that has been lost in popular vocabulary and perhaps renounce my personal campaign to bring *hearken* back into style. Even so, I do believe it would benefit us all to remember and consider what it means not just to show up and be present, but to stretch toward, to regard with care, curiosity, and eagerness all that God has placed in our lives. Imagine a world full of women who refused to just show up, but instead attended to all that Christ called her to. I want to be that kind of woman, friend. Let's be those women.

Amnesiac

A strange thing happened in 2020. The world ran out of toilet paper. As is the case with most of life's big or bizarre events, I remember exactly when I first heard the news. Do you? A friend of ours told Ross and me about it. Apparently our nearest Costco was completely out of toilet paper and people were flocking to grocery stores to snatch up the rest of the supply.

We live in a rural town, a good half hour from any city with a Costco. I had just been to our local grocery store, where the shelves were fully stocked. We laughed that those big(ger) city folks must be going a little crazy in the time of COVID, and we went about our business. The following week, the joke was on us, as not a single store around had toilet paper in stock.

The run on toilet paper reached far beyond my small corner of the world. Scarcity plagued Singapore, Japan, India, Australia, and many other countries around the globe. In Hong Kong it was reported that an armed gang robbed a local store of six hundred rolls of toilet paper in one day.[7] Numerous stories surfaced of physical altercations between shoppers, neighbors, and even family members, duking it out over toilet paper. The world did indeed go a little crazy.

Jokes about the crisis abounded, and everyone seemed to be asking the same question: *Why toilet paper?* For all of the threats a global pandemic may have posed, a run on toilet paper seemed to catch everyone by surprise. While international shipping and supply chains were certainly impacted by the pandemic, in the United States, 99 percent of tissue products are produced within our own borders.[8] Our toilet paper supply was never at risk. As interesting as that may be, I found it far more interesting to learn that this wasn't our first toilet paper shortage. Did you know that?

In 1973, not too many years before I was born, the world was experiencing an energy crisis due to an OPEC oil embargo. Rising prices and supply shortages began to plague the American economy, putting consumers on edge. In December of that year, comedian Johnny Carson lightheartedly read a newspaper article in his opening monologue, which posited misinformation about a potential shortage of toilet paper. The article struck panic in the hearts of Carson's 20 million viewers and, within days, the United States was experiencing its first legitimate toilet paper shortage. In the grips of fear and under the threat of further loss, Americans made a mad grab for the security, for the hope of normalcy, that toilet paper seemed to provide.

As we all nervously laughed at the toilet paper jokes of 2020, chiding the ridiculousness of it all while keeping any eye out for when and where we might be able to replenish our own dwindling stock, it is fascinating to know that this was not indeed unchartered territory. It was not a foreign response. Nonsensical panic had created a run on paper products in the past. We were asking questions we should have had answers to, but we collectively forgot. And then we laughed about it. That is worth considering.

Centuries ago, a not entirely different group of people struggled with their own fear-driven responses. The Israelites suffered greatly under an oppressive regime, and the scars from their wounds seemed to have a pulse all their own. Consider that, friend. We aren't all that different. In time, the whole tribe of them escaped captivity and their captors were annihilated in their wake. It was no small miracle. This newly liberated people were off to claim new ground, a new heritage in a land well suited to them. But they tired on the journey. They became impatient in the wait. They forgot the miracle that had become their deliverance, the miracle that had been their provision, and the hope of what lay ahead. They forgot their God.

Instead of stretching toward what was ahead of them—the God who had literally been going before them for years now, answering and providing in miraculous ways—they balked under the burden of their present concern.

"What have you done to us in bringing us out of Egypt?"[9] the Israelites cried when they saw the Egyptians pursuing them to the Red Sea.

"Would that we had died by the hand of the LORD in the land of Egypt,"[10] they spat as they sat hangry in the desert.

"Why did you bring us up out of Egypt, to kill us and our children and our livestock with thirst?"[11] they demanded when they became parched on the journey.

Their faith crumbled in their failure to remember God's ways, who He is, and how He loves. Doubt gave way to fear, and they began to long for captivity again. It's heartbreaking to read, isn't it? It's even more heartbreaking to live.

God tenderly taught the Israelites the importance, the greater magnitude, of His work and provision, continually asking them to remember this day and to pass this lesson on to their children.[12] The psalmist did just that. In Psalm 106 we read an earnest retelling of the Exodus story.

> Our fathers, when they were in Egypt, did not consider your wondrous works; they did not remember the abundance of your steadfast love, but rebelled by the sea, at the Red Sea. Yet he saved them for his name's sake, that he might make known his mighty power.[13]

Do you see it? The Israelites failed to remember God's way, who He is and how He loves. That became the story that was told of them. But the story of God is being retold and remembered by the psalmist here. Since we know the story, if we skim just the subject and verbs in the next few verses, we can learn His ways in a surprisingly clear way:

He rebuked the Red Sea . . . (v. 9)
he led . . . (v. 9)
so he saved . . . (v. 10)
and redeemed . . . (v. 10)

This psalmist opened his song boldly with praise. "Praise the LORD!" he says. "Oh give thanks to the LORD, for he is good, for his steadfast love endures forever!"[14] Despite the forgetfulness of the psalmist's own forefathers, the story of God remained true, and future generations would praise Him for what He did. What mercy! But I wonder how many valleys of doubt and distraction the Israelites could have avoided if they had chosen to pause and remember. I wonder how many of those same valleys we might avoid.

Double Whammy

Look, friend, I am not saying that forgetting about a toilet paper shortage is akin to forgetting God. Don't read that. But the world as we know it is oriented toward this present moment like never before. We have access to news and more news and new news and what would have never previously been considered news, every second of every day. The world trades in novelty, and slowing down to actually consider what we attend to, what every so-called minor moment of our lives is stretching us toward, takes counter resistance. It takes effort. It takes memory.

Neuroscientists are strides ahead of us here. In a research article for the Department of Psychology at Yale University, researchers addressed the interactions between attention and memory. "Although it is more common to think about how attention improves memory, there is growing appreciation for how memory optimizes attention and perception."[15] The interplay here is interesting. We cannot remember what we do not first attend to, but memory plays a key role in guiding and directing, in "optimizing" attention.

As believers, we are called to be people who set our minds on things above.[16] We are called to remember God and stand firm, and we are called to love God with our minds, which must demand the very attending and memory-making capabilities that He has designed within us. Do you see how this works? He has created us for the very obedience He called us to. In adoration, we get to use the faculties of *His* design to honor Him, to bring Him glory. By His power, He has given us everything we need for life and godliness,[17] even with our aging brains, even in a world of seemingly endless distraction, even when it's harder than ever to pay attention. We do not have to be a people who fail to remember. There is another option.

but then she remembered . . . to attend

This section is something unique and different, friend. It's my favorite part of the book, where the words that lay flat can begin to take form in *your* heart and mind. Remembering is not an isolated act; it is recall for a purpose, recall that changes us, directing and realigning our hearts with what is true. Don't skip this part. After each chapter you will find space to answer some related questions. These questions will take you directly to the Scriptures, helping you process these ideas in light of God's Word. Take the time to engage with the thoughts and ideas we just discussed and filter what you have read through Scripture. It will require you to attend to God's Word. Please do not resist the time it will take. This is likely the most important part of the book.

Okay, just state it. How quickly did you figure out the word *hummus* before I did in the opening story? Were you even stumped *at all*?

It's humbling to bump up against the limits of memory! **Where do you currently see the most obvious limitations of memory in your own life?** Here's a list to get you thinking:

I mix up my kids' or other people's names. Y N

I forget why I walked into a room. Y N

I lose my phone or keys regularly. Y N

I have forgotten calendar events or appointments. Y N

Past dates, years, and events easily slip my mind. Y N

I am liable to forget the name of random words like
    hummus. Y N

How do you respond to these limitations?

What is your immediate reaction or reflex when you misstep in remembering, when your memory feels fuzzy or temporarily fails you altogether? Do you find it funny or frustrating?

Do you feel ashamed, concerned, indifferent, or another emotion altogether?

Our responses are indicative of our beliefs, so it is wise to consider them.

Let's think about the roots of attention for a moment. If attention comes from the infinitive verb *to attend*, which is derived from the Latin *attendere*, the literal root means "to stretch toward." If you could zoom out on your life, viewing it as an outsider, almost like *you* were one of the baby zinnia starts on my windowsill, what would you see your life is stretching toward?

The thought of *stretching toward* reminds me of Paul's words in Philippians 3. Take a few minutes to read Philippians 3 carefully.

What does Paul count as loss (v. 8)?

Because of the surpassing worth, value, or excellence of what (v. 8)?

These passages give us a frame of reference for Paul's heart and his resolve. William Blake is famous for saying "We become what we behold." What would you say Paul is beholding?

Paul admits that he has not obtained perfection, but that he presses on, making every effort. Why (v. 13)?

Do you believe the same thing is true for you?

Now take a look at Romans 8:31–39. In your words, use the space below to write the gospel, the good news, in this passage.

See this, friend. In Philippians, Paul is pressing on—we must be pressing on—toward what has been graciously afforded to us through salvation, the finished work of Jesus Christ. We can be conquerors in the challenges of this life, *more than conquerors* even amidst our very real imperfections and shortcomings, even in the struggles and hardships of this life, through the inseparable love of God (Romans 8:39). **How could attending to this truth and remembering it shape our daily struggle?**

Finally, let's look at Philippians 3:13–14 one more time: "Brothers, I do not consider that I have made it my own. But one thing I do: forgetting what lies behind and straining forward to what lies ahead, I press on toward the goal for the prize of the upward call of God in Christ Jesus." **What is the "it" Paul is referring to when he says, "I have not achieved it" (Philippians 3:13 NLT)? Look back at verse 12 in your Bible if you need help.**

Paul hadn't achieved it and neither have we. Take a deep breath, friend. Too often we carry a burden, living under the shame of imperfection that we aren't made to bear.

What one thing does Paul choose to focus on (vv. 13–14)?

Forgetting the past of his own mistakes, his own misdeeds, his own failed attempts, in light of the present, he strains forward. The Greek word here is *epekteinomenos*. That sounds fancy, or perhaps odd, or both. It's only used once in all of Scripture, and I don't expect you to remember it or spell it or even say it. (How is that for a book on remembering?) But here is what I want you to know: According to Matthew Henry, the word literally means "to stretch yourself toward."[18] That is sounding familiar now, isn't it? Henry says Paul is "bearing towards his point: it is expressive of a vehement concern."[19]

This is what Paul is calling the church at Philippi *and us* to. Stretch toward what lies ahead. Don't get bogged down with perfectionism, or even worse, the appearance of perfectionism. Press on because Christ has made you His own. Forget all that His forgiveness has covered and strain toward, stretch yourself out toward, what lies ahead, the upward call of God. This is maturity in the life of the believer. We are made to live toward Him. Let's stretch, friend.

2

beginning with what we must know

Sometimes I don't remember the people I know and love, *rightly*. Perhaps that sounds odd, particularly when they are living and active right alongside me. But the truth is, we all wrestle with misguided remembering at times, even when it comes to the people we love most. On the daily it might look something like this: My husband makes a comment that lands sideways with me, that doesn't necessarily offend me in the moment, but it raises a silent question for me—a question I barely know exists.

Throughout the day, if I replay the conversation, the question starts to materialize and bring other questions to the surface. It might come out something like, *Why would Ross ask how I'm doing with my current writing deadline? Is he worried I'm not going to finish in time? Does he think I can't do it? Why is he doubting me? It is not helpful to have a spouse who doubts your ability to get the job done. Why can't he be more supportive?* Just like that, on a tough day when my own doubts have likely primed the pump,

I can spin a story from a simple question to one that will land Ross squarely in the camp of the unsupportive spouse, without his even knowing it. It's an unfair game to play. Everyone loses. And yet, with spouses or coworkers, with adult children or parents, extended family or friends, too often we play.

A few years back I remember mulling over just such a question one day, letting it roll around until I was good and irritated, and I talked to Ross about it that evening. The particulars of the perceived offense evade me now, but the outcome—the most important part—is seared in my mind, because I was wrong. I completely misjudged his question and intentions. Ross is not perfect, and neither am I. (That should be stating the obvious, but occasionally when reading books we don't remember the author *rightly* either. I will risk the obvious to remind you here, we're both sinners saved by grace.) Even so, the overwhelming body of evidence from our twenty-plus years of marriage has established the fact that Ross is good and loyal and supportive and kind. While that is true, I can still at times be tempted to spin a story *and believe a story* that is completely contrary. It's uncomfortable to own that, friend. I am sometimes tempted to believe the worst of people. At my worst, I'm tempted to presuppose all kinds of generalization fallacies, even regarding people that I love. Realizing this begs the question—if I can assume the worst of others, do I also at times assume the worst of God?

The Obvious Answer

When I was writing my first book, *I Choose Brave*, everything was new for me. I had never written a book before. My dad had a major health crisis. And the world was experiencing a pandemic. New, new, new. A few weeks before the book was set to release, I remember the pressure mounting. There were podcast interviews peppering my calendar, mixed in with writing deadlines, a social media schedule, and book launch check-ins. Absolutely none of this was normal life for me, and I could literally feel a ball of nerves forming in my stomach. I'm not typically anxious. This nervous indigestion was also new for me, and I didn't like it.

I messaged my friend Kelly and told her exactly how I was feeling. I told her how there seemed to be so much ahead, so much that would need to be done, and so much of it that couldn't be done right now. I didn't like the impending anxiousness of it all, and I asked her, "Is this just what I'm going to feel like for the next six weeks—a ball of nerves all the time?" Kelly messaged me back immediately and offered me words that I will never forget. "Katie, I'm going to ask you one question: What are you believing to be true about God right now?" Kelly was brave enough to go right to the root of my unbelief. I sat in my parked car listening to her message that afternoon and I bawled because I knew the answer to her question, and I hated everything about it.

Right remembering can only result from right belief. A. W. Tozer famously said, "What comes into our minds when we think about God is the most important thing about us."[1] That's a weighty concept to consider, isn't it? It's foundational. What comes into our minds when we think about God is what we believe to be true of Him. Recalling what we believe to be true of Him is how we remember Him. And how we remember God directly impacts how we orient ourselves in the world. But in a world bidding for our attention, a world teeming with distraction, how *do* we remember God, and even more important, how do we remember Him *rightly*?

Start Here

We cannot remember what we do not first know. That seems obvious, right? The word *remember* comes from a Latin root that means to call to mind or recall, which is to *bring back* to the mind. Our memories are complex and still somewhat mysterious agents. Various regions of the brain sort, file, and store all kinds of data in a myriad of ways. But remembering is retrieving that data and bringing it to the "front" of the mind. Our brains are intricately designed for both successful storage and retrieval, but on their own they cannot retrieve what they have not first stored. We cannot recall that which we have not learned.

In Philippians 3, Paul begins the last half of this letter to the church with a list of reminders. He states his repetitive intentions blatantly: "To write the same things to you is no trouble to me and is safe for you."[2] That is worth considering in and of itself. Being reminded of truth was a safeguard for the church then, just as it is for us today. But what truth did Paul want to remind them of? What may be considered the key verse in all of Philippians and the heart of Paul's life and ministry: "Indeed, I count everything as loss because of the surpassing worth of *knowing* Christ Jesus my Lord."[3]

Paul was imprisoned when he wrote those words. He experienced tangible loss. He goes on to say that he had suffered the loss of all things and he counts them as rubbish—"garbage," some translations say (stay tuned, we'll dig deeper into that word in the remembering section at the end of this chapter)—"that I may gain Christ . . . that I may *know* him and the power of his resurrection, and may share his sufferings."[4] He reminded the church at Colossae that they have put on the new self, "which is being renewed in knowledge after the image of its creator."[5] This same old truth that Paul thought wise and safe to remind the church of was to know God and be changed by that knowledge. He was willing to count everything else as worthless compared to knowing God. That's a powerful commitment, isn't it?

And here's why—because what we *know*, what we believe to be true, has immeasurably far-reaching implications. *Knowing* someone brings a certain level of comfort. When you engage with someone you know, your interactions will be more casual or familiar compared with someone you don't know. Take my friend Candee, for example. She has been my close friend for many years, and she's my neighbor (as far as country neighbors go), so we do a lot of life together. We know each other well. And knowing her changes how I engage with her. Our conversations are less the light-switch variety with a clear on and off, and more a steady stream. I would never leave Candee a voicemail and say, "Hey, this is Katie," because she knows my voice and no introduction is necessary. When you know someone, familiarity replaces formality.

But knowing someone doesn't only change your engagement with them in the present; it changes the full dynamic of your engagement. Every story I hear of Candee's past, before I knew her, is intrinsically filtered through the lens of what I know to be true of her today. Likewise, any prediction or expectation I could make about the future will be based on what I have known to be true of Candee in the present. Knowing Candee rightly, knowing her fairly and honestly, is essential because it will impact everything I assess to be true about her in the past, present, and future. If our earthly relationships in our fallen and failing and redeemed state can be so greatly impacted by our *knowing*, how much more will our full and never-ending knowing of Christ—the immutable Savior of our souls—be impacted by what we believe be true of *Him* in the past, present, and future? If, as the Westminster Catechism states, the chief end of man is to glorify God and enjoy Him forever, then we can see why Paul began with knowing Christ and being renewed by that knowledge, being changed by it. Remembrance can only begin after we first *know*.

A Deeper Well

In our Instant Pot world, we have learned to shave time from every task because we are people in a hurry. But knowing doesn't happen overnight. We want it to, but part of the beauty of *knowing* is the time it takes to know. Part of the beauty of knowing

God is that He is far more than our minds can possibly bear understanding.

To the church in Rome, Paul exclaimed, "Oh, the depth of the riches and the wisdom and the knowledge of God! How unsearchable his judgments and untraceable his ways!"[6] With awe, Paul looked upon God's greatness, His wisdom and understanding so far beyond our own. This is the God Paul was willing to count absolutely everything else as loss to know. In Isaiah 40, the author spends the entire chapter trying to convey the immeasurable greatness of God: "Who has measured the Spirit of the LORD? . . . Who made him understand? . . . Have you not known? Have you not heard? The LORD is the everlasting God, the Creator of the ends of the earth."[7] You can almost see these men reaching for better words to communicate who God is. He is unknowable and yet He invites His people over and over again throughout Scripture to know Him, to return to Him, because of His steadfast love for them. *For us.* Can you see it? These are His ways, who He is, and how He loves. We need to *know* all of it.

A beautiful and heartbreaking demonstration of this invitation throughout Scripture comes to us via the story of the Israelites. We scratched the surface of their story in the previous chapter, but there is far more to mine. The plight of the Israelites is often so familiar to us that we trivialize its importance, but there is much we can know about the character and nature of God through their story. In Deuteronomy 6 we meet Moses as he is teaching the Israelites in preparation for their journey into the Promised Land. He is calling for their obedience, that they may fear the Lord. "You and your son and your son's son, by keeping all his statues and his commandments."[8] The forethought here should catch our attention and give us pause. It's countercultural. The world seeks to orient us toward this present moment, but God supersedes the present moment with a hope and a future, a vision far beyond our present moment. Tim Mackie of the Bible Project says, "Moses challenges them with his wisdom and warning because he doesn't want these Israelites to repeat their parents' mistakes. Rather, he invites them to respond to God's grace and mercy with love, faithfulness, and obedience."[9] Did you catch that? This is not only wisdom for generations; this is a wisdom that requires a response. God is giving His people truth that must be tended and remembered and passed on.

Moses's instruction will become known as the Shema, the repeated prayer of the Jewish people and words Jesus will declare in the gospels as the first and greatest commandment, to love the Lord your God with all your heart and with all your soul and with all your might. And because he has led these people, and he knows these people, Moses tells them, "You must commit yourselves wholeheartedly to these commands that I am giving you today."[10] Is there any greater way for a loving Father to acknowledge the frame and tendency of His children in light of the seriousness of His command? *Wholeheartedly*, Moses tells us. Commit yourself to this, to knowing and loving God. But this God of the past, present, and future doesn't stop there. He tells His people they must pass this truth on, to teach their children and talk about it all the time. So when the bounty of God's blessing is upon them, they do not forget. "Who brought you out of the land of Egypt, out of the house of slavery. It is the LORD your God you shall fear. Him you shall serve and by his name you shall swear."[11] Do you see it, friend? God is saying in it and through it and after it, in plenty and in want, you must *remember me*.

Pontiacs Worth Picking

This past spring I stood waiting for Ross at the feedstore. My hands were chock full of garden seed packets—most of them flowers, which is just about right to me—while he reached for a brown paper bag to load up some seed potatoes. It was the cusp of gardening season and they said seeds may be in short supply. We don't really know who *they* are, but we listened and made sure we had what we needed to sow hope into the soil as soon as the weather turned.

As Ross glanced over the five or six potato varieties piled in wooden bins that looked as if they'd been cradling seed potatoes for generations, an overall-clad farmer asserted himself. "Red Pontiacs!" The farmer flung his words with certainty. "Those are the ones you want." Ross smiled in his easy way, welcoming the interjection. "Those are the good ones, huh?" "You bet," the farmer replied quickly. "My mom always planted Red Pontiacs. She'd plant a row of potatoes, a row of carrots, and a row of peas. When we'd harvest 'em, she'd cook 'em all up together and cream 'em. It doesn't get any better than that."

I took a closer look at the farmer. His overalls were worn soft, as was his skin. I would guess he was in his seventies. I don't even know what creamed potatoes are, or how they differ from mashed potatoes, but this farmer had both the shape and sense of a man who had eaten his share of them. He had Ross and me sold on the Red Pontiacs, but he wasn't done. "We grew up in Alaska, you know. My mama, she'd plant a whole row of tomatoes and cook 'em down into sauce. She'd start that sauce right after breakfast and let it simmer all day long. Then at dinner she'd fix the noodles and mix the whole thing together. It doesn't get any better that. I've tried for years and never once made a tomato sauce as good as hers."

I was done thinking about potatoes. I was with the farmer in his childhood kitchen with his mama. I was wondering about a tomato sauce so rich in flavor, rich in care, rich in love, that a grown man, a grandpa farmer, stands in a feedstore and the very goodness of the memory just pours out of him to strangers. I like to cook, and bake even more. I can make a pulled pork dinner that will have my family coming back for seconds, and a cinnamon roll that is a standard birthday request. But have I ever made a meal that will be remembered when I'm gone? What is the essence of a meal that could nourish my kids long after they leave my home or the memories of which will fill their hearts and overflow to others, even in a feedstore? That is a pretty good meal.

While he may have thought so, it was likely never really about the meal for that man—creamed potatoes or tomato sauce or whatever—it was all just a conduit. It's no surprise that his attempts to replicate his mama's food were futile, because it was the love and care of his mama that made it all lovely. It was the home and the hard work and security of it all that nourished him. His mama's good food was richly seasoned by her provision for him, and knowing her food was knowing her, a knowledge that has served his heart well beyond her years of service. Do you see it? It's a beautiful analogy of the way our God loves and provides. The way the lasting truth of His character is seeded deep into us that it might be poured out into those after us. We get to know the nature of the immeasurable and transcendent God through His provision, His Word, His history, His Creation, and His engagement in the lives of those around us. We must know Him to remember Him, and when we remember Him, we can pass the truth of Him on, even in a feedstore.

The Little Issue of Distraction

So if knowing God is foundational and remembering Him can only come as a result of knowing Him, what are we to do about the thick weeds of distraction that become constant roadblocks? What if we want to know Him, but consistent Bible reading is *hard* and our prayer life is inconsistent at best? What if we want to set our mind on Him but it also feels like there are a hundred other legitimately important things that take up our brain space as well? Sure, we all get caught up in nonsense scrolling from time to time, we can admit that. But what about the less obvious distractions—when our minds seem to scroll without permission, when every pause brings us back to an impending or upended conversation? What about uncertainty in the economy, indecision about the future, and when anxiety over the news dominates our thoughts? What about when struggles with our children, our parents, our spouse—people we are charged to love—capsize our quiet time? How do we possibly fight all these distractions to remember? Let's begin with a story, a little science, and then something tangible.

I once accepted a challenge from a friend to not eat sugar for thirty days. You could call it a sugar fast, I guess. I eat pretty healthy most of the time, and I'm always up for a challenge, so it took little persuading for me to commit. I was convinced I could manage this pretty easily. And I did, until I got hungry. It wasn't the it's-time-for-dinner hungry that was hard. It was the in-between or bored hungry that proved to be difficult. It was the "I don't really know what I want so I'll go stand in the pantry" hungry that was a bit more challenging. I stared aimlessly at the pantry shelves and instinctively wanted something sweet because, well, sugary snacks are an easy default, but also because I wasn't supposed to eat sugar, so my brain seemed to fire off, "Don't eat the sugar. Don't eat the sugar! DO NOT EAT THE SUGAR! SUGAR! SUGAR! SUGAR!" If this makes no sense to you, then you have clearly not done a sugar fast. But I was determined and succeeded at overcoming the screaming in my head. I ate chips instead.

Here is where the story gets interesting, friend. I don't even care much about chips. I wouldn't say I don't like them because what's not to like about chips? I will eat them. But I don't love them. I'm indifferent toward chips and will easily let them go stale in the pantry. Until I am deprived of sugar, apparently. Then, in desperation and despair, I will grab those chips and hope like everything they aren't stale. Honestly, it might not even have mattered if they were stale at that moment.

The point here is not my eating habits. The point is, we are naturally good at finding loopholes and workarounds. We are quick to apply a surface solution to remedy a problem, but in doing so, we often fail to address the heart issue behind both the problem and the solution. Jeffrey Hall, University of Kansas communications professor, recently published a first-of-its-kind study assessing how we use our time during social media fasts.[12] His means and methods were far more scientific than my own little sugar fast, but interestingly enough, his results weren't all that different. His findings showed that decreased social media consumption did not result in increased interpersonal interactions. Meaning, less social media did not lead to more real-life engagement, in the same manner that my sugar fast did not necessarily equate to better overall eating habits.

Instead, participants in Hall's study ended up surfing the web more or doing other work they had been putting off. "Spending time on social media is not going to make your life a whole lot worse or a whole lot better," Hall concluded in his study, "because the things most strongly associated with having a good day and feeling good throughout the day—like sharing a meal or spending time with close friends and family—don't seem to change whether people are off of social media." While Hall's conclusions may still be up for debate, he makes an interesting point here. It is unwise to assume that removing a distraction or negative input from our lives (sugar or social media, for example) means that we will automatically fill that void with something positive. If we want to be distracted, if we want to avoid hard things, if we want to zone out or fill ourselves with some cheap and easy junk food, we will. We are capable of ripping off a Band-Aid, only to replace it with another one.

Instead of Distractions

Even so, what if the distractions themselves aren't the real problem? Dr. Margie Warrell, writer and board member for Forbes School of Business and Technology wisely states, "It would be convenient to blame distractions on undermining our ability to finish tasks efficiently, perform at a level we know we are capable of, or even focus on what we need to prioritize on any given day. But more often our *productivity levels* (measured in terms of what we accomplish in any set period of time) *are impacted less by the distractions themselves, and more by the fact that we have simply not been clear about what we really want to focus our attention on*" (emphasis mine).[13] I think she's on to something very important here, friend. For the business students and for us.

Think about this. When we are aimlessly scrolling the internet—following an Instagram rabbit trail, stalking a friend of a friend, or maybe shopping for things we don't even need but have somehow been enticed by—no one needs to tell us to pay attention. We can drift and wander in full focus of a hundred unimportant things with no problem whatsoever. The truth is, we are pretty good at paying attention to what we really want to pay attention to. I could ignore the incessant questions from a whiny child and waste ten minutes of my life reading the earth-shattering celebrity news that jumped across my screen, and no one would have to tell me to focus on that. Have you ever thought about that? We don't become easily "distracted" from our distractions.

This is exactly the point that Dr. Warrell is making. Perhaps the myriad of distractions isn't so much the problem. They make an easy scapegoat in our blame game, but we seem to find a way to focus on what we really want to. What if we have simply not been clear about what we really want to focus our attention on? Interestingly enough, an article in the *Berkeley Economic Review*, discussing the attention economy, closes with similar wisdom: "As we continue to drown in a surplus of stimuli trying to capture our attention, perhaps we must focus on paying attention to what we pay attention to."[14]

I'm using secular sources here because I think it's important. The whole world believes we have a distraction issue. Business

marketers, stay-at-home moms, students and career profession-
als, believers and unbelievers—the attention economy does not
discriminate; it wants the attention of everyone. And yet profes-
sionals working in this area of expertise, by means of common
grace wisdom, are pointing to some pretty solid solutions. What
if instead of managing our distractions, we considered simply
getting clear on what it is we really should be paying attention
to? Here's where we are going to part ways with secular business strategists, because we are living for a far different gain.
Our motivations cannot be the same, and thus, ultimately, our
solutions cannot be either.

Settle Here

In her book *Disciplines of a Godly Woman*, Barbara Hughes shares
a beautiful story of a young woman who had newly come to know
Christ.[15] Carol was her name. Carol immediately joined a wom-
en's Bible study and sat, with her borrowed Bible, next to a group
of women who had spent years there. If Bible study was a sport,
these women would have lettered in it. They were varsity and
Carol was the rookie. Carol mostly listened as the pros answered
questions and discussed, but eventually, when the conversation
quieted, she summoned her courage and spoke up. "I found the
most wonderful verse last night!" Her words tumbled out with
clumsy, pure delight. She carefully thumbed to the place marked
in her Bible and began to read aloud to the rest of the group with
all the awe and reverence she believed the Scripture deserved.
"For God . . . so loved . . . the world . . . that . . . He . . . gave . . .
His one . . . and only . . . Son . . . that whoever . . . believes . . . in
him . . . shall not perish . . . but have eternal life."[16]

   Can you imagine Carol—so new and young in the faith—
finding this verse that just seemed to capture all of what she
finally understood to be true? Can you imagine how sacred,
how precious it must have felt to read those words, believe those

words, for the very first time? This is exactly what John New-
ton was getting at when he penned those now-famous "Amazing
Grace" words: "How precious did that grace appear, the hour I
first believed." It was *that* precious to Carol. The story goes that
there was not a dry eye in the room when Carol was finished
reading. Carol's unadulterated awe for the gospel was contagious,
and every woman around her was humbled and reminded, *This
is our faith. This is our God. Do we remember?*

We all desperately need the reminder of the treasure we hold,
the gift of grace that has been afforded to us. *This* is what we
must pay attention to. We need to see the Giver rightly, again
and again. We need to hear the stories of who God is, what He
has done, and how He has loved throughout time and Scripture,
throughout our lives, throughout the past, in the lives of our
friends yesterday, today, and tomorrow. He is unchanging. And
these deep and vast wells of remembrance exist for us to drink
from, that we might not only be reminded, but that we might
once again pay attention.

When the Remembering Is Hard

It might seem easy to remember a mama who tended the fresh
veggies and creamed 'em good, an Alaska childhood with scratch-
made tomato sauce simmering all day long. That must be nice.
If such novelties were a far cry from your own childhood, you
might bristle at the contrast. I don't blame you. The effects of
malnourishment leave real scars, and the remembering can feel
spoiled. But perhaps truth, a *right* remembering, can be more
helpful than we give it credit for.

It was important to Jesus that His disciples knew Him rightly.
They had walked with Him and had seen His power. But long before He commissioned them to go and make disciples, He asked
them outright, "Who do you say that I am?" Peter answered
clearly, "You are the Christ, the Son of the Living God."[17] And

Jesus was pleased. He acknowledged the blessing Peter possessed not because of an earthly inheritance, a truth spoon-fed to him, but because this was truth the heavenly Father had revealed to him. As believers, the same truth has been revealed to us, and our answer should mimic that of Peter. *You are the Christ, the Son of the Living God.*

When we look back and our stories are pocked with scars, we can see the reality of pain through our present redemption and know it still to be true—*You are the Christ, the Son of the Living God.* When our past is filled with the repercussions of our own poor decisions that long outlive the moment of their making, and shame would like to suffocate, we can remember in light of truth because He *did* redeem even us. *You are the Christ, the Son of the Living God.* When the injustice was real, when innocence was robbed, and the remembering feels like drowning there all over again, we remember in light of the One who grieves *with* us, made a way *for* us, bore the price of our freedom, and became grace that changes it all—past, present, and future. Even here we can proclaim what was, is, and will always be true: *You are the Christ, the Son of the Living God.*

I want to challenge you to remember rightly, friend. For some of us, that must be done with the help of wise and godly counselors who can help us navigate deep waters of pain with the wisdom of Scripture, with truth. If you are there, ask God for the courage to do so. Ask your pastor for leadership in finding a counselor who can help lead you well, not to just unearth the past, but to remember who God was, even there. And for the rest of us, those moving so fast in the present that we fail to take time to remember who God *was*, even in our past, there is a feast of fruit we are neglecting. The history of His presence, His faithfulness, and His mercy in our past might be entirely missed, never fully reaped, if we fail to look back and see His goodness over the timeline of our past.

Historical revisionism is a popular controversy in our world today. We can argue long over its impact on the large scale, but what if we considered its impact closer to home? How often do we give it sway in our own lives, in our own stories? In our failure to look back to the hard, *through the hard*, to see Christ's steadfast love there, we risk allowing a different story to be remembered, to be retold. If I fail to see Christ in my past, that directly impacts how I honor Him in the present and what story I pass on in the future.

In Psalm 139, we read of the psalmist doing this in real time, trying to convey the vastness of who God is relative to the psalmist's past, present, and future. Matthew Henry calls this psalm a devout meditation "upon the doctrine of God's omniscience, which we should therefore have our hearts fixed upon."[18] In the words of the *Berkeley Economic Review*, we might say this psalm is calling us to "pay attention to what we are paying attention to."[19] The psalmist's meditation comes out in beautiful phrasing, not the least of which is "Wonderful are your works; my soul knows it very well."[20] And in the margin of my Bible I have a whispered reminder inked in my own scrolling script—*"I need my soul to know it very well."* His works, past and present, are wonderful. It's who He is. And we desperately need that truth to wash over not only our current days but every past and future day as well. This is a maturity of faith. This is remembering rightly.

I discovered this in a subtle and yet glaring manner recently when talking with my own children about the house we built almost a decade ago. It's a lovely home on a small acreage that serves our family (and allows us to serve others) well. As housing prices have risen drastically in our area, I was recently commenting on how we likely couldn't even afford to build our own home today if we were just starting out. The thought of that startled my kids a little, and questions and discussion and stories ensued, the heart of which was the timing of building our home. Before building, we waited and saved, and planned to wait some more, until some wise and trusted mentor friends encouraged us otherwise. Their advice caught us by surprise because we admired their own careful stewardship of their finances. We assumed that continued patience and saving would be prudence they agreed with. And they did, but they also understood the careful stewardship of time. "You're in good shape," they advised us. "And your kids won't keep. Build your home." And so we did. We heeded the wisdom of godly mentors and sought to steward well. This home, the timing of it, the finances it required, the size and space and everything about it have been nothing short of a blessing to our family.

Now, that's just one little story in our family history, but I was surprised my children never knew it. They lived it, but they were younger then and weren't always aware or perhaps we didn't share all the details of what was taking place. But they aren't young anymore. And if I don't tell them the story of God's faithfulness to our family, that might not be the story that gets passed down. A story of my husband's hard work may assume the narrative. Maybe we'll be credited with real estate savvy and expert timing that really wasn't the case. God's goodness is the story of our home. It's my job to remember that truth, to see God in the past and pass that story forward.

Do you see how simple and yet how powerful this is, friend? Let's see Him. Let's remember Him and pass truth on. *He is the Christ, the Son of the Living God. May we have souls that know it very well.*

but then she remembered . . . to remember rightly

Part of the beauty of family is familiarity. It's built right into the word. Family is typically comfortable because you are known there. But part of the *challenge* of family is also familiarity. The same can be said of marriage, perhaps some friendships, or even coworkers. When we have a rich history of relationship, we have a track record that is hard to escape. At our worst, we all commit the generalization fallacies mentioned in the beginning of this chapter—when one comment causes us to quickly assume the worst about someone.

Can you relate to this in any of your own relationships?

Sometimes we give strangers far more courtesy than we are willing to give the people we know and love. Are there people you love that you don't always remember rightly?

What about God? What are the areas of your life where you don't remember Him rightly?

If remembering rightly begins with knowing rightly, as we discussed in this chapter, how would you currently rate your knowledge of God?

How are you actively pursuing knowing Christ?

How much do you value it?

Let's return to Philippians 3 in your Bible and read verses 7–10 carefully to see how much Paul valued knowing Christ. I've read this passage many times, friend, and it still astounds and confounds me. I love Paul's steadfast decision, and yet I squirm a little when I turn the question on myself. Do I count everything else as a loss in comparison to the excellency, the surpassing, not-even-comparable value of knowing Christ? I hope so, but our hearts are prone to wander. Asking this question is a good check-in.

What might you be valuing more than knowing Christ? I believe this is a question our heavenly Father loves to help us answer; He loves to meet an earnest heart here. Below is a list of common competitors. Circle the ones that apply to you, and feel free to add your own as well.

My home	Food
My marriage	My children
My friends	Comfort

Freedom	Reputation
Physical fitness	Personal time
Security	Finances
Self-image	Health
Career	Politics
Goals	Serving
Education	Image

Knowing *about* Christ instead of knowing Christ

The tone of Philippians is heartfelt, an exhortation to a body of believers that Paul knows and loves and is not afraid to shoot straight with. In chapter 3, verse 8, Paul says he has suffered the loss of all things and counts them as *rubbish* (some translations say "garbage") in order that he might gain Christ. The word for *rubbish* here is an interesting one. In the Greek it is *skybalon* (pronounced scuba-lawn), and it is used only once in all of Scripture. A word like this is always interesting to me because it means it is unique. Of all the familiar words the author could have chosen, inspired by the Holy Spirit, he selected *this* one.

But what does it mean? While biblical scholars and translators like to argue on this a bit, there is strong evidence that the words *rubbish* and *garbage* have been selected as a play to our "English sensibilities." According to parallel ancient texts, the Greek word used here comes with more emotive, almost vulgar, connotation as it is often used in reference to human excrement or animal dung. I don't know about you, but I live in rural farmland. There are words around here for that, and *rubbish* isn't one of them. Now, you may be wondering, *Why does it even matter?* Because the contrast here is what Paul is getting at. He has suffered the loss of all things he tells us in verse 8, good and lovely and beautiful things—comfort and friendship and freedom and health—and he counts that all as *skybalon,* as dung, in comparison to knowing Christ. The incredible contrast is what the author is getting at. *Christ is that much greater.* And we must remember it.

In what areas of your life are you feeling loss right now? Review the list we just looked at. Perhaps some of the items you circled will provide clues. Where are you feeling the struggle, things not quite as they should be?

It is common—normal, even—for us to feel loss when things we care about fail. When our kids hurt, we hurt. When our marriage is off, everything is off. When I watch my aging parents age, it can feel like loss. *It is loss.* But Paul paints a contrast that is full of hope even here. He is not asking us to consider our kids, our careers, or our aging parents as *skybalon*. He is reminding us that the surpassing worth of knowing Christ even in our suffering and loss is impossible to overstate. Even when the loss is real, we cannot afford to forget the surpassing worth of knowing Christ.

Can you pause and attend to Christ here? Can you invite Him nearer that you may know Him more fully, that your soul may know Him well, as the psalmist said in Psalm 139?

Right now, I encourage you to stretch toward Him, to ask Him by His Holy Spirit to remind you of His surpassing worth, especially in the midst of what you are standing in, even if it's just lifting your eyes and with courage that only comes from Him, saying, "God, help me know you more." That takes courage, friend. But this is how we stake our claim. **Use the space below to write your own prayer to God. Declare what you know to be true of Him and invite Him to keep reminding you.**

What are you believing to be true about God right now? This is the question I want to sear in your mind, friend. This is the SOS I want to be ready on your lips when despair or fear or frustration weighs heavy. I now work to make this question, and its honest answer, my reflex. Like David did in the psalms, we can pour out our honest heart to God and He'll help us realign our feelings and hearts with what is true. This question is a tool, a great way to begin that conversation.

What are you believing to be true about God right now?

Sometimes the remembering is hard. The past can feel like a minefield of mistakes we would much rather forget. But for those of us who have accepted the saving grace of Jesus Christ, our story cannot help but be rife with His mercy, because it is the story of what we have been saved from and for. Take a minute to think back on the timeline of your life. **In the space below, plot out a simple timeline of your years, labeling as many major events and turning points as you can.**

Where might you need to ask God to redeem your memories, to help you see He was faithful? We love to sing loudly about how great His faithfulness is, but sometimes we forget to even notice it! Looking at your timeline, what stories of His faithfulness do you need to remember? What stories do you need to be active about passing on?

3

actions that bring us back to remembrance

On September 1, 2019, I received one of those phone calls we all dread. My mom was straining to steady her voice on the other end of the line, metering her words carefully, as if I might be a toddler walking too close to a cliff or dancing my finger toward a light socket. I could tell instantly that her words were important but that she didn't want to scare me. Good moms never stop mothering. Perhaps we only get better at recognizing their faithfulness as we ourselves age.

My dad was having chest pains, likely a heart attack. He and my mom were at the ER. This phone call would tattoo our time-line. We didn't know it yet, but this moment would become a fixed *before* and *after* in the life of our family. We would come to regard events and memories as either *prior to,* or *since* this day. Even so, it wasn't the scare we thought it was. It was birth pangs.

The evening before, my parents had celebrated forty-six years of marriage with a family dinner on my back patio. Our cheeks glittered with storytelling tears and laughter as twinkly lights held back the night. But darkness was nearer that we even knew. A few days later, my seemingly healthy dad would be wheeled back for an emergency quadruple bypass surgery. That surgery saved his life, and yet healing did not come as the medical team had hoped. Instead, my dad languished in the hospital week after week after week. Lifesaving can be heartbreaking.

My dad was finally sent home with a milrinone infusion pump he would now wear every minute of every day. The pump was attached to a PICC line, which delivered life-sustaining medication straight to his heart. *Sustaining* was the key word, and there was increasingly less life to sustain. And then we were sent to see the big-city specialists.

I remember so vividly the first time my dad heard the words "Mr. Leaverton, we would like to talk to you about a heart transplant." The tenured team of physicians, all in their long white coats, gathered around the meeting table using practiced and steady tones to make their case. There wasn't much of a case to make; my dad's options were few. After they had delivered a fair number of facts, they slowed their pace and asked my dad if he had any questions. He sat motionless for a second. Then his eyebrows rose, he folded his hands, and he slowly said, "Yes, I do. Can you tell me what you mean exactly by a *heart transplant*?"

A tidal wave of compassion erupted inside me for my dad in that moment. It singed my throat, stung my eyes. *This* was far more difficult than watching a great man leveled with a broken heart, hooked up to a wiry mass of tubes in the ICU, his mobility minimized to mere shuffling when he even found the strength to walk. This was remembering.

Sometimes a song or a taste or a scent will bring you instantly back to another time and place. Sometimes a sterile medical office and softened words delivered honestly by a white coat doctor will do the same. *"You have lost all your amniotic fluid. Without amniotic fluid, your baby's lungs will be unable to develop.*

I'm sorry." I had once before been the recipient of serious words that I couldn't quite comprehend, didn't want to believe. I had sat in silence, mentally begging for the truth not to be true, a figment of my imagination, dramatic hysterics. I had ridden a roller coaster and thought it was over only to realize the scariest part was just ahead. Remembering changed my listening here. It changed my heart. And in the weeks and months ahead, I would learn, it changed everything.

Remembering Is Not Static

In his second letter, Peter tells believers that as long as he is around, his goal is to *stir them up* by way of reminder.[1] Some translations say "to wake them up" or "refresh them." Whichever translation we choose, it is obvious that the reminder is the impetus for action. Stirring up by way of reminder produces something. It forces what has become stagnant to emulsify. It activates. When I pour heavy cream into my steaming cup of dandelion tea (it's oddly wonderful, I promise), the cream bobs heavy, coagulates almost, until I stir it. The disparate parts meld together in the stirring and my creamy decaffeinated concoction results. It needs to be stirred. Remembering is that sort of action; it stirs.

The Hebrew word for *remember* is *zakar*, and it is used frequently throughout the Old Testament. *Zakar* first appears just after the wrath of God has been poured out upon mankind due to their wickedness and complete corruption. For forty days floodwaters pounded the earth, and "[God] blotted out every living thing that was on the face of the ground."[2] And in Genesis 8:1 we are told, "But God *remembered* [*zakar*] Noah and all of the beasts and all the livestock that were with him in the ark." In the midst of the torrent, God remembered. This very first mention of remembering in the Bible refers to God. Isn't that a bit surprising?

In modern English we tend to define *remembering* in contrast to what it is not. Remembering is the opposite of forgetting, we might say. But is it? Did God *forget* Noah? When, as the New Living Translation puts it, "all the underground waters erupted from the earth, and the rain fell in mighty torrents from the sky,"[3] had God sort of forgotten about that faithful man He called and sought to save, the one who walked with Him, the one who He said He would make a covenant with? Did God stand at the door of the ark and close it, effectively tucking in Noah and his family with a vast array of animals, and in five short months accidentally forget about him? Let me answer that for you. No, He did not. God did not forget Noah, and He does not forget us. Our understanding of the word *remember* might require a little more insight. When God said via Isaiah, "Can a mother forget her nursing child? Can she feel no love for the child she has borne? But even if that were possible, I would not forget you!"[4] not only did He mean it, He gave us insight into His nature that we must keep in mind.

We can learn more of the full meaning of *zakar* if we read a little further in Genesis 8. Immediately after God remembered Noah, He made a wind blow over the earth and the waters subsided. His remembering was a call to mind and a call to mercy. God's remembering was action. We see this same thing in the following chapter. In Genesis 9:15 God says, "I will remember my covenant that is between me and you and every living creature of all flesh. And the waters shall never again become a flood to destroy all flesh." His remembrance comes with action; it comes with mercy.

We find the same to be true when *people* remember, when they *zakar*, in Scripture. In Genesis 40 we meet Joseph in prison. Honored by his father and then dishonored by his brothers, honored in Egypt and then dishonored by Potiphar's wife, we meet Joseph on yet another loop of the roller coaster that was his life for many years. In prison he interpreted the cupbearer's dream favorably and then humbly requested, "Only remember me, when it is well with you . . . to mention me to Pharaoh."[5] Joseph wasn't asking for the cupbearer to simply call him to mind and not forget him; he was requesting mention, mercy, favor. He wanted a remembering that came with action. Are you beginning to see the difference? Remembering is not static. We sell remembering short when we define it as the opposite of forgetting. Remembering is compelling. It is tied to action. Our remembering becomes our doing.

Been There, Done That

This is one of my least favorite phrases—*been there, done that*. I suspect this is a personal bone to pick and has very little wholly righteous underpinnings, but I am fully convinced that A) it has been so overused that it offers nothing to progress a conversation, and B) it frequently comes off as dismissive of the person it is lobbed toward. I suppose it could be used in a sense of camaraderie or validation. It could possibly mean "I empathize with your plight. Yes, I've made the same mistake or had similar struggles." But to me, more often than not, it rings of one-upmanship. Like, "Nothing to see here!" Like lazy shorthand that really means your story is not unique or original, barely even interesting, and certainly not worth me wasting real sentences, real conversation, on. *Been there, done that.*

I may be supposing a little too much on an innocuous phrase. It is possible I overthink it. But there is one area when it can be incredibly useful—when it is directed toward *our* past, rather than in response to others. When current events and present circumstances trigger reminders that, *Oh, wait, we've been here before*, they become the conduit through which we can choose to see God, triggers by which we attend to Him. *Been there, done that* in this context can call us back to remembering how God worked and how He loved in the past. Remembering His character and

His unchanging nature steadies our faith in the present. Because we *have* been here before, we can remember that He was there too. We can remember His mercy and provision, His intimacy and His timing. We can remember the ways He sustained us, forgave us, brought community, and ministered to us in deep hurt by the power of His Holy Spirit. We can remember that *He* has been there, and *He* has done that.

No doubt our pulse will quicken when hard news comes. Our minds will stir and questions will arise. We may desperately want to Google for answers. We may want to refresh our newsfeed until we wear a blister on our finger because we want answers; we are hungry for some kind of update. But when we force our minds to pause and remember, *God with us, the One who was and is and is to come, even here, even now*, we change the pace of things. We activate our faith by remembering. When we reach for real truth, real stories of His faithfulness in our lives, in the lives of our friends and family, in the stories of the faithful throughout history, we are choosing to link our present concern to the God who has been faithful throughout all of time, and we call our faith to account.

The Israelites, who we studied a little in chapters 1 and 2, had this same kind of experience on many occasions. Sometimes they were better at employing the *been there, done that* than others, but I love the parallel that we see in their water crossings. In Exodus 14 we find the whole tribe pinned against the Red Sea with Pharoah's troops charging toward them. We know how the Israelites responded. They were a wreck. They freaked out—or "feared greatly,"[6] in more biblical terms. They called out to God in complaint and declared it would have been better for them to have stayed in Egypt. But half a chapter later, after God parted the sea and overcame the Egyptians, we learn that the Israelites saw the great power of God that day, that they feared the Lord and believed Him.[7] God had been there and He had done it. And they knew it to be true.

If we skip to the book of Joshua, we find that Joshua has now taken over the leadership role for the Israelites as Moses has passed on. Or Josh was subbed in for Mo, as I might affectionately say when I retell the story to my kids. To which they would either snicker or roll their eyes, depending on the day. Anyhow, wouldn't you know that this massive tribe of people, about two million or so of them, are blockaded by a body of water once again. This time it is the Jordan River they are up against. Joshua knows this is the route, and long before Michael Rosen took us on a bear hunt,[8] Joshua knew that the *only* way was through it. But this time, when he told the Israelites to get ready, the people didn't balk. According to Scripture, they said to Joshua, "All that you have commanded us we will do, and wherever you send us we will go. . . . Only may the LORD your God be with you, as he was with Moses!"[9] This is solid remembering, friend. This is maturity. They know the Hero of their past. They remembered what God did and how He loved. They didn't need to freak out with worry. Remembering truth steeled their hearts with courage for what was ahead. And once again, when they were ankle-deep in it, stretching out just a bit further in faith, God parted the waters. Again.

I love that story. I love the way God brought His people back to a familiar place and whispered remembrance over it all. I love how a history with God changed this stubborn people and everyone around them. Because they knew God's ways, who He is and how He loves, they moved forward in faith this time. They paid attention to Him, kept their eyes on Him, and weren't thrown into a tailspin of distraction and doubt by the very real problem in front of them.

God has given us a beautiful picture of similitude here, perhaps because He wants us to see the contrast clearly, but life doesn't always present the same set of circumstances twice. The point isn't necessarily the similarities, but the constant: Remembering God changes things. Whether you have experienced His profound goodness in a devastating diagnosis, His beyond-understanding peace in the ache of grief or loss, His provision in despair, or His love in loneliness, it all adds up to a track record of knowing Him that becomes a deep well to draw from. Every journey we take with God should add to the storehouse, and *remembering it* activates our faith when our world spins wild.

Stepping-Stones

Let's pick up where we left those Israelites, full of faith, fueled by remembering on the banks of the Jordan River. They were on their journey to the Promised Land and had taken the long route there. God intended to provide for His people and consecrate Joshua's leadership by showing He was *with* Joshua, and when the Israelite priests stepped into the water, God cut off the flow of that flooded river and stood it up like a wall, the New Living Translation says (see Exodus 14:29). Miracle done.

The Israelites crossed the Jordan on dry land, but God had more than His people's present providence in mind. God always has more than our present providence in mind, friend. Joshua chapter 4 tells us that when the entire nation of Israel had finished crossing the Jordan, God told Joshua to command one man from each tribe to take up a stone from the riverbed. "'Take twelve stones from here out of the midst of the Jordan, from the very place where the priests' feet stood firmly, and bring them over with you and lay them down in the place where you lodge to-night.'"[10] It was a very specific request with a very specific intention. Joshua later moved those stones to their camp at Gilgal and explained to the people, "When your children ask their fathers in times to come, 'What do these stones mean?' then you shall let your children know, 'Israel passed over this Jordan on dry ground.'"[11] Matthew Henry wisely states that "God's mercies to our ancestors were mercies to us; and we should take all occasions to revive the remembrance of the great things God did for our fathers in the days of old."[12] This is exactly what is happening here. The stones were to revive remembrance of what God did, but their purpose didn't stop there.

If we keep reading in Joshua, we learn even more. "For the LORD your God dried up the waters of the Jordan for you until you passed over, as the LORD your God did to the Red Sea, which he dried up for us until we passed over, so that all the peoples of the earth may know that the hand of the LORD is mighty, that you may fear the LORD your God forever."[13] Joshua is articulating this clearly so that God's people may know and remember and retell this story rightly. *Get you some stones as reminders. Stack those things up where it is obvious, so that your kids will ask about it. And when they do, tell them. God was there and He did it. He did it at the Red Sea and then He did it again! Don't be tempted to think it is because you are good or strong or brave. God is mighty and God did it so that the earth may know, and you may fear the Lord your God forever. Because God did it.*

I can almost hear the fire in Joshua's words as he so desperately wants these people (and us) to know and remember and pass on truth. It was God's command that the Jordan be split dry in two for His people. And it was God's command that these men pluck stones straight out of the Jordan as a reminder. God had been there and done that. And it was with compassion that He wanted to help these people, with their feeble minds and distracted ways, to have a physical reminder of what He had done so they could keep passing it on. Do you see how good He is, friend?

A Feast to Remember

I love following themes through Scripture, noticing and noting how God engages His people, how He provides, and how He loves. We can learn much of the character and nature of God simply by watching His engagement with His creation. One such theme I've been noting for some time is that of food—specifically eating. The Bible speaks of meals of celebration and abundant feasts, meals of sustenance and survival and hospitality. Our physical need for nourishment is never overlooked by God, and the way He engages those needs tells us much of His character —much that we are now trying so hard to remember.

In the garden of Eden, God created a bounty of food for Adam and Eve to enjoy. Wayne Grudem points out in *Systematic Theology*, "Since there was no sin in that situation, and since God had created them for fellowship with himself and to glorify himself, then every meal that Adam and Eve ate would have been a meal of feasting in the presence of the Lord."[14] Isn't that beautiful to think about? We love the fellowship of shared meals; they strengthen our families and become a means of connection— both physical and relational nourishment. And all of this stems from our original design to feast in the presence of the Lord. We were made for that.

Because of our sin, for the time being, that specific feasting is not available to us in the same way. As believers, we have received the reconciliation of Christ, but we find ourselves in the already but not yet. In our waiting, we look forward to another feast in the presence of the Lord at the Marriage Supper of the Lamb. John writes about this in the book of Revelation, when he hears "what seemed to be the voice of a great multitude, like the roar of many waters and like the sound of mighty peals of thunder, crying out, "Hallelujah! For the Lord our God the Almighty reigns. Let us rejoice and exult and give him the glory, for the marriage of the Lamb has come, and his Bride has made herself ready."[15] Can you even imagine—those words of worship pouring forth from so great a multitude, so many faithful believers, it is just roaring with the power of crashing waves, like peals of thunder? That will be some feast. John says, "And the angel said to me, 'Write this: Blessed are those who are invited to the marriage supper of the Lamb.' And he said to me, "These are the true words of God.'"[16]

Do you notice how our Bibles open and close with feasts and fellowship in the presence of our God? What a beautiful picture, a beautiful frame for God's redemptive story. But He did not leave us without means of communion here in the in-between. He set up a plan for active remembering, a shared meal of remembrance that has roots rich in the history of His continued provision. He gave us the Lord's Supper.

To more fully understand the history here, we need to go back just prior to the final plague in Egypt. The Lord revealed to Moses and Aaron how His plan for their deliverance was going to unfold. Every Israelite household was instructed to sacrifice a male lamb without blemish, wiping some of its blood on their doorposts and lintel so that when the Lord came during the night, He would *pass over* their home and their firstborn would be spared. This would be their present provision, but God never stops there. His present provision is always drenched with future purpose as well. As He was giving them this instruction, He was also carving a path for future remembrance. "This day shall be for you a memorial day, and you shall keep it as a feast to the LORD; throughout your generations, as a statute forever . . . for on this very day I brought your hosts out of the land of Egypt. Therefore you shall observe this day, throughout your generations, as a statute forever."[17] This became what we know as the feast of the Passover, a memorial feast celebrated to remember the way God had delivered His people. But even more, it is a foreshadowing of an even greater deliverance yet to come.

Fast forward with me over fourteen hundred years to another Passover celebration. When the hour had come, Luke tells us Jesus and His apostles reclined at the table. Jesus said, "I have earnestly desired to eat this Passover with you before I suffer."[18] Can you see His heart in these words? Jesus knew what was immediately ahead for Him. He knew he would *be* the Passover lamb, sacrificed for the deliverance of mankind. And before it took place, He longed to just be with His people.

Dr. Sinclair Ferguson says, "[Jesus] loved what the Passover meant. He loved what it meant to Him personally. But he also loved what it meant to him in history."[19] The richness of remembering, of foretelling, of the consistent truth of God's nature and Jesus's deep desire for obedience were all very near to Him in this moment, and as the hour neared, He desired to be with His people.

In a sermon on this passage of Scripture, Ferguson shares of a time he and his wife were away at an extended-family occasion. His four adult children were at this event as well, but none of their families were able to attend. The original six Fergusons made arrangements to dine together one evening, and as they gathered, one of them suggested that they sit around the table in the same places they had sat all those years gathered around their own family table. Ferguson shares, "I think that probably will mark one of the happiest hours of my life. When, as it were, *all* the blessings of the past and family life—the fellowship, the fun, the struggle, the ordinariness, the failures, the successes, the loves, the commitments, the devotions, the growing—it was almost as though they were all consummated in this moment around this table, around this meal. These were the ones I loved most of all in the world and I had looked forward to this occasion with deep longing."[20] As a mother nearing the launching stage of parenting myself, I love the picture that Ferguson paints for us. In anticipation I can understand his joy. We cannot begin to comprehend the weight of the suffering Christ was about to endure, but we do know what it is like to earnestly enjoy being with our people, don't we?

Paul recounts Jesus's words from that evening spent sharing the Passover meal with His disciples. "The Lord Jesus on the night when he was betrayed took bread, and when he had given thanks, he broke it, and said, 'This is my body, which is for you. Do this in remembrance of me.' In the same way also he took the cup, after supper, saying, 'This cup is the new covenant in my blood. Do this, as often as you drink it, in remembrance of me.'"[21] His heart heavy for the cost of what lay in front of Him but grateful to be with His people, Jesus would become the link between the old and new covenant, the Passover lamb, and in doing so He instructed us in a sacrament, an ordinance, that would serve as a tangible reminder of our communion with Him even today. The Lord's Supper is our feast, our act of remembrance, a thanksgiving for the great cost of our salvation. "*Do this* in remembrance of me." Jesus specifically commanded us *to remember.* Once again, it was active, present provision drenched with future purpose.

In Matthew 26:26, as Jesus sat with His disciples in this re-membering feast, He instructed them, "Take, eat; this is my body." When we partake in communion, as Grudem says, "As we individually reach out and take the cup for ourselves, each one of us is by that action proclaiming, 'I am taking the benefits of Christ's death to myself.'"[22] This isn't only remembering what Christ did; it is remembering what His sacrifice *does.* It reconciles. This is a remembering that involves all our senses and requires action. This is *zakar.* Matthew Henry brings this all together for us beautifully. "This bread that was *broken* and *given for us,* to satisfy for the guilt of our sins, is *broken* and *given to us,* to satisfy the desire of our souls. And this we do in *remembrance* of what he did for us, when he died for us, and for a *memorial* of what we *do,* in making ourselves *partakers of him,* and joining ourselves to him in an everlasting covenant; like the stone Joshua set up for a *witness.*"[23] Communion is our witness. It is our doing because of what He did. It is our memorial to remind us, to discuss with our kids and grandkids. It is our active remembering.

An Older, New (Wo)man

I hope you are beginning to see how this active remembering is threaded and woven throughout Scripture. We may have long overlooked it or trivialized it in familiarity, but these accounts and many more were written long ago, in former days for our instruction as Paul told the Christians in Rome,[24] so that we might be encouraged toward perseverance and endurance through the Scriptures, even now in a world that places great importance on the power of the present. In a world that capitalizes on our weakest yearnings to know and be known, God has implemented and utilizes the beauty of His own design, human minds created to remember, to faithfully call us to pay attention, to faithfully call us back to himself. I have another example of active remembering that I want to share with you.

I was baptized for the very first time at the age of forty-one. That would be wonderful and quite expected had I come to know Christ at the age of forty-one, but I have known Christ nearly my entire life. So this is where my baptism story, while equally wonderful, becomes a little messy. I was never baptized. And I have no reasonable excuse.

I was raised in the church. My dad was a pastor and I was in the pew pretty much every Sunday growing up. The churches I was raised in were small—many just a handful of families in rural areas—so baptisms were a rare occasion. And I slid under the radar. I don't recall avoiding baptism intentionally, although I'm sure I had a normal amount of apprehension about a public dunking. But I also don't remember fully understanding the importance of it. It seemed almost optional to me, so I opted out.

In my late teenage years, I remember my parents realizing their oversight in shock. "I can't believe we never had you baptized!" they said. Their choice of words was likely accidental, but they were met squarely with my teenage rebellion, and I instantly committed: "No one is *going to have me baptized.*" The hardness of our hearts can lead us down roads we never intend to travel, friend. And so, I wasn't baptized.

As time went on, by the grace of God, I outgrew my teenage rebellion. As a young adult I met Christ anew. I began to understand relationship with Him like never before, and I finally sought to fully seek and follow Him. Baptism occasionally caught my attention, but I also believed it was for new believers—"repent and be baptized," you know. I messed that part up. I missed out, and now the baptism services at my church seemed primarily for children about nine years old, or for brand-spanking-new adult converts with awesome stories of Christ's transforming work in their lives. A forty-year-old woman who has led and served for years seems a little out of place in that lineup.

During the pandemic, my church received the blessing of a new pastor. Pastor Cliff led our congregation through those choppy waters, including mask mandates and vaccine opinions. That is no small feat for a pastor new to the congregation. He sort of started from scratch with us, reteaching some of the fundamentals of the faith and reminding us of the truth of God's Word. And he got serious about baptism. He reminded us why it was important. He swung wide the doors of invitation for anyone, *everyone*, ready to proclaim Christ, to choose to be baptized, and for the first time I recognized that invitation included forty-one-year-old women who knew Christ but chose the foolishness of rebellion many years ago. It included people who felt they missed their chance, were "too old," or somehow "too churched," to find a path to obedience. *It included me.*

Grudem says, "There is a blessing of God's favor that comes with all obedience, as well as the joy that comes through public profession of one's faith, and the reassurance of having a clear physical picture of dying, and rising with Christ and of washing away sins. Certainly the Lord gave us baptism to strengthen and encourage our faith—and it should do so for everyone who is baptized and for every believer who witnesses a baptism."[25] There is a lot to unpack there, but it's worth doing. Baptism is a clear picture of dying and rising with Christ, of Him washing away our sins. It is a physical act of remembrance, a choice we don't soon forget. It is a present provision with future purpose. It is *zakar*—remembering that embodies action.

When I shared a photo of my baptism online, my friend Tim told me that baptisms make him cry every time. That is exactly the strengthening and encouraging of our faith that Grudem says happens when believers witness baptism. We rejoice in the believers' own dying and rising with Christ as we are *reminded* yet again of our own. I'm with Tim. Baptisms make me cry too, just as mine did on that Sunday in May when the Holy Spirit finally humbled my heart toward obedience. I too get to rejoice through tears with every believer who obediently chooses God's sacramental act of remembrance. My sins, they are many, but His mercy is more.

Baptism is an outward expression of an inward decision. It symbolizes the regeneration that has occurred in our hearts by the grace of God. It is not necessary for salvation, "But it is necessary if we are to be obedient to Christ, for he commanded baptism for all who believe in him."[26] We see the command throughout Scripture: "Repent and be baptized every one of you in the name of Jesus Christ,"[27] was Peter's clear call in his bold sermon at Pentecost. In the Great Commission Jesus told His disciples, "All authority on heaven and earth has been given to me. Go therefore and make disciples of all nations, baptizing them in the name of the Father and of the Son and of the Holy Spirit."[28] Paul told the church in Galatia, "For as many of you as were baptized into Christ have put on Christ."[29] God's Word does not overlook baptism. Neither should we.

If you have accepted Christ's salvation and been baptized, rejoice in the act of remembrance He has given you. Remember that day and celebrate with every believer who comes behind you, choosing the same. If you have chosen Christ and somehow skipped the baptism part, learn from me. We don't get to skip out on obedience. As we tell our children, delayed obedience is no obedience at all. But even so, God is full of mercy here. I've tasted it. Know that the invitation to obedience is doors swung wide—nine-year-olds, new adult converts, forty-one-year-old women, and you. It is time for every believer to participate in this holy act of remembrance. I, for one, will be celebrating with you.

Getting Active

I hope you are beginning to see it, friend. Remembering is how we pay attention to God in a highly distracting world. Through Scripture, He has given us a framework of remembering, a pattern for it, and instructed us in sacraments that we are to be active about. Remembering is, perhaps, a looking back so that we can move forward in truth. It's recognizing that God has been there and done that, and calling that truth to mind as fuel, as confidence, in who He is today and will still be tomorrow. We may be traveling the unexpected loop on another roller coaster. We may hear of world news that threatens our stability. We may be on the receiving end of a phone call we pray we will never receive. But we know who God is, and choosing to remember Him here changes everything.

but then she remembered . . .
remembering is active

Let's try a short-term memory trick and see if we can be some sort of memory master, just for fun. Below is a random list of words. Don't look at them yet! Set a timer for two minutes and try to memorize as many of the words as you can in that time. After the time is up, give yourself another two minutes to write down as many of the words as you can. Ready?

Nine	Swap	Cell	Ring	Lust
Plugs	Lamp	Apple	Table	Sway
Army	Bank	Fire	Hold	Worm
Clock	Horse	Color	Baby	Sword
Desk	Grab	Find	Bird	Rock

According to research, the typical storage capacity for short-term memory is seven, plus or minus two items.[30] How did you fare?

Moving on from random words, let's take a look at some words with a *little* more staying power. Hebrews 4:12 tells us, "The word of God is living and active, sharper than any two-edged sword, piercing to the division of soul and spirit, of joints and of marrow, and discerning the thoughts and intentions of the heart." *These* are powerful words. Take a couple minutes to read through 2 Peter 1 and get an idea of where you are in the Word.

Who wrote this book?

To whom was it written?

What are you some things that catch your gaze? What is the author trying to communicate?

What does this chapter tell us about God?

Don't be afraid to look up words you are unfamiliar with. Greek and Hebrew roots are great for in-depth study, but sometimes it is helpful simply to read the passage in a different translation to get a better idea of what the text is saying.

You knew I could not write a book on memory without challenging you to memorize, right? *It's time.* **I challenge you to memorize 2 Peter 1:3–8. I know it's a chunk, with a list. This is tough, friend. But it is good for your heart and your mind. Begin by writing it out below and then again on a sticky note or a 3x5 card, something portable.** Tell a friend for accountability. Better yet, ask them to memorize with you!

Memorization is what we hold when we don't have a Bible with us. The work of it forces us to meditate on God's Word. The effective effort makes the Word become our words, it shapes what we share and how we pray. I cannot recommend Scripture memorization highly enough. For some reason, we often only encourage it to children, but we should never outgrow it. Your brain is designed for this. Be patient with yourself, but make it work!

Let's think through communion and that beautiful idea of feasting and fellowship in the presence of God. That is what we were created for, but we are so far removed that it is sometimes hard to even wrap our brains around the idea here. Open your Bible to Genesis 1 and read verses 27–31. Can you even imagine what fellowship with the Lord was like then? Give it a try. What might feasting in His presence have been like?

Move over to Genesis 3:8–13. How did fellowship in the presence of God change?

Now move to the very back of your Bible, Revelation 19. Read verses 1–10. Describe what the author heard.

How are the reactions different from what you just read in Genesis 3?
In verse 9, who does the angel say is blessed?

A return to feasting and fellowship in the presence of God is what awaits every believer. Full restoration means full communion with Christ once again. In communion, we pause in gratitude to remember the cross and Christ's sacrifice. We remember the source of our redemption, and we look ahead to the feast that awaits us because of His finished work. We remember with purpose that moves our hearts toward Him. *Zakar.*

Have you been baptized?

Do you have any photos you could look at from that day? Photos serve as beautiful reminders of important events that we are quick to forget.

If you were baptized at an age when you were old enough to remember, what conversations or encouragement led you to that decision?

Take a few minutes to think back on that day. If you were baptized as an infant and have no memory of your baptism, if possible, maybe you could have a discussion with your parents about that day in your life and they could share about the preparations or ceremony that went with it. Baptism is an important memorial in the life of the believer!

If you are a parent or grandparent, I want to encourage you to share your baptism story with your kids. This is the stuff they need to know. This is truth about their heritage that we want them to remember.

If you haven't been baptized, or if you, like me, have ignored the scriptural command, I'm going to ask you to pray about it right now. Talk to your pastor about it. If you feel ashamed or embarrassed, I promise I get it. But I also know we serve a mighty God who forever welcomes His children's obedience. The gates of invitation are swung wide, friend. Even now. Even for you. I'm cheering you on.

4

who you are and how you were made

My daughter, Bailey, started ballet at the age of three, and she danced for many years. She was long past the learning-to-walk stage when she began dancing, but she was still in some of those feet-fumbling years where learning to skip is mostly the class goal and gracefulness is hardly an option. Those early years are the cutest years of ballet. It was shortly after her foray into dance that the work of artist Edgar Degas caught my eye. A French impressionist from the 1800s, Degas created numerous paintings of dancers, and I thought it might be lovely to hang one of his prints in Bailey's room someday—a little artistic inspiration for my own tiny dancer.

A few years later, during a homeschooling art unit, we began to learn more about who the painter Edgar Degas was. He was born into wealth and took to art at a young age. He sketched and painted and sculpted with a particular affinity for the female form. Although he was among the Impressionists, he liked to stretch toward realism and considered himself independent. But while Degas frequently chose to paint female subjects, many sources credit him with being a misogynist, being unkind and degrading to the women he worked with, referring to them as animals. Degas never married, and in his later years retreated from both art and life as his eyesight and hearing failed him.

Knowing the artist changes the art a bit, doesn't it? Degas's work is still lovely, there is no denying his talent. But there is a grit to it I can't unsee now. I feel compassion for the ballerina in the painting. Was she mistreated? And if so, did she feel like she had no other option than to pose for a famous artist? Did she not know she was worth more?

Is it *too* honest to just admit I didn't really want to write a chapter in this book on identity? So much has already been said on the topic. If I have heard it spoken of at least a hundred times, then I know you likely have as well. We hear it from pulpits and platforms, from speakers and in song. But we also hear it in the world, in the news, and in politics, and it can all become a bit confusing. What *does* it mean exactly—my *identity* is in Christ? If identity is a form of rootedness, a definition of who you are and the grace in which you stand as a believer *because of what God did*, then it is worth knowing and *remembering*, so we can live that truth out fully for the glory of God and the good of others.

On our journey through this book, we began with knowing and remembering who *the Artist* is because we realize that knowing the artist changes the way we view the art. We had to start there. And we also studied the active nature of remembering, how it impacts our doing. Now we are going to look at how it impacts our being. Remembering who we are because of *Whose* we are is essential to how we carry out our mission. It is essential to how we pay attention to God in a loud and distracting world.

What Is *Not* Helpful

Last year a mentor friend of mine, Deon, was discussing identity with her daughter, Cassie, who is a millennial. Deon and I had recently been having iron-sharpening-iron conversations about identity—questioning and challenging and spurring one another on—and she thought it would be interesting to get an opinion from someone in a different age bracket. "What are *your* thoughts on identity?" Deon asked Cassie during a long car ride to a family ski trip. Cassie responded honestly. "I think it's important. It affects everything. I've heard a lot of Christian women talk about it, and they always say, 'Your identity needs to be in Christ,' but ultimately, that's not all that helpful."

Cassie's thoughts stuck with me for days, weeks. *Identity is important. It affects everything. Everyone is talking about it, but ultimately it's not all that helpful.* How is that possible? If identity seeks to ground us in truth, root us in a firm foundation of who we are because of Christ, and the message is being communicated relentlessly, why is it not all that helpful? Cassie's honest insights spurred me to study even more. First, let's start at the very beginning, because as Fräulein Maria would say, it's a very good place to start.[1]

A Brief History

The root of the word *identity* comes from the Latin word *identitatem*, meaning "sameness." Does that surprise you as much as it did me? I would have thought *identity* alluded to uniqueness, but sameness? It's interesting and also a tad bit confusing. *Identitatem* is directly translated in English to the word *identity*, and its derived definition of *sameness* has been the prevailing formal definition since its original usage sometime in the sixteenth century. Modern dictionaries as recent as the 1990s have relied on this definition of sameness, although in more recent history identity has taken on a much different practical meaning. While many dictionaries still include *sameness* as a lesser used definition for *identity*, academic sources have moved to a different definition completely. The American Psychological Association, for example, defines *identity* as "an individual's sense of self defined by (a) a set of physical, psychological, and interpersonal characteristics that is not wholly shared with any other person and (b) a range of affiliations (e.g., ethnicity) and social roles."[2] Political Science Professor James D. Fearon of Stanford University posits that identity is the "socially distinguishing features that a person takes a special pride in or views as unchangeable but socially consequential."[3] Words are powerful, and those definitions are worth reading carefully.

If this appears to be a fair distance for the definition of a word to travel, you are observant. And not alone. Even secular scholars join us in questioning the mutability of the definition of *identity*. And it has traveled that distance in a very short amount of time. According to Philip Gleason's commonly noted journal article titled "Identifying Identity: A Semantic History," "The historically minded inquirer who gains familiarity with the literature, however, soon makes an arresting discovery—identity is a new term, as well as being an elusive and ubiquitous one."[4] Fearon says, "Identity is a new concept and not something that people have eternally needed or sought as such. If they were trying to establish, defend, or protect their identities, they thought about what they were doing in different terms." These observations were fascinating to me. Somehow identity is both new and common, popular. The concept tends to lack history and roots and appears to be elusive. These insights come from scholars inside the world of academia, but they ring true with what we see inside the church.

We are void of sermons or Christian literature even mentioning the concept of identity in ages past. We have no word from the reformers, nothing from the Puritan preachers, and nothing from the great revivalists of old. In fact, the word *identity* does not even appear to have entered the church until the late twentieth century, and not gained full acceptance until around the year 2000. Interestingly enough, CNN reported that dictionary.com declared *identity* to be its 2015 word of the year. "The trends that

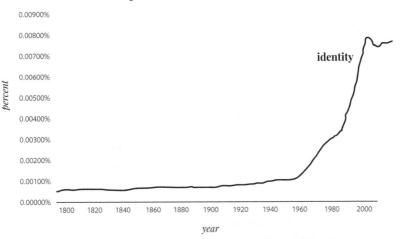

Occurrences of the word *identity*
in printed books 1800–2019

we saw linguistically all point to a larger shift in the way society thinks about identity as being more fluid, which was evidenced by the increase in related events and news headlines,"[5] states the CEO of dictionary.com. Apparently, the world and the church were both coming of age at the same time in regard to identity. That is worth noticing. Take a look at the charts above and below which, according to Google Books, show the prevalence of the word *identity* and the phrase *identity in Christ* in books from the years 1800–2019. The data confirms the surprisingly recent popularity of the terms.

What is even more interesting is that you will be hard-pressed to find the word *identity* in your Bible. A few modern translations may include a mention or two in the Old Testament, but you will not find the expression *identity in Christ* anywhere at all. The etymology of words and phrases is helpful to know at times, particularly if we are building a biblical principal without a biblical word for it. Does that make it wrong? Not necessarily, but it can make it confusing. If you go to your Bible trying to sort out a concept that has shifted from sameness to uniqueness, a concept that has become highly influenced by the world and culture around us so much that it was recently deemed the word of the year and you can't even find that word in Scripture, it *is* confusing and, perhaps, in Cassie's words, not all that helpful. Now, why does this matter in a book about paying attention? Because in the land of distraction, the currency of trendy and nuanced terminology does not seem to provide the anchor we hope it will. We are more vulnerable than we realize. Seemingly harmless inputs sometimes land square, lodge deep, and in the midst of distraction, we find ourselves prone to forgetting *who we are*. We are prone to forgetting that we have been bought with a price and created for a purpose. When a glimpse of another life, a healthier marriage, a tidier home, and cleaner kids catches our gaze, or a marketer shows us slimmer thighs and cuter clothes, these distractions of our eyes can easily become distractions of our souls. They become a direct hit, a temptation for a lie we slowly, silently begin to believe about who we are, or even

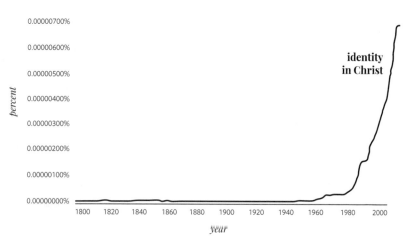

Occurrences of the phrase *identity in Christ*
in printed books 1800–2019

more often, who we are not. That is why we must pay attention, friend. That is why we must remember the truth of God's Word here.

So here is how I want to unpack this. *Identity* is kind of a complicated and messy word. We addressed that. It's not wrong. It's pretty new, but for much of the church, I believe its usage is based firmly on the truth of God's Word. However, I think we can do a better job of bringing this concept from the spiritual realm and into the practical. So your identity is in Christ—great!—but what does that *mean*? In the following section we are going to discuss who we are because of who Christ is, and I'll try to get really practical about what that means for us right now as believers trying to pay attention to Him while we are at home in the world. Our identity has real implications, and I want us to get a crystal-clear grasp of it here.

Foundational

The secular definitions of identity almost always revolve around a sense of self, but this language stands in opposition to the language of the gospel. As believers, our sense of who we are is inextricably linked to who Christ is. We know that the fear of the Lord is the beginning of knowledge,[6] and the heart of who we are must exist in direct submission to Christ. Consider these Scriptures:

> Ah, Lord GOD! It is you who have made the heavens and the earth by your great power and by your outstretched arm! Nothing is too hard for you.
>
> Jeremiah 32:17

> Here there is not Greek and Jew, circumcised and uncircumcised, barbarian, Scythian, slave, free; but Christ is all, and in all.
>
> Colossians 3:11

Because Christ is my foundation, my hope is in Him. Not the news. Not the results. Not my ability to grind or produce or perform.

Because Christ is my foundation, my future is secure. Do you believe it? News *will* come. Nahum said, "The mountains quake before him; the hills melt; the earth heaves before him, the world and all who dwell in it. . . . He knows those who take refuge in him."[7] I can feel the quake and shake of life on this earth and yet live with certainty that my future is secure.

Unchanging

If our identity is in Christ and He is immutable, our identity is necessarily unchanging too. As James says, in Him there is no variation or shadow due to change,[8] and the same must be true of an identity rooted in Him. That is hard to wrap our minds around in this ever-changing world, but it's important for us to remember.

> Jesus Christ is the same yesterday and today and forever.
>
> Hebrews 13:8

> "For I, the LORD, do not change."
>
> Malachi 3:6

Because Christ is unchanging, I don't have to fear change. I don't have to fear life's transitions. I don't have to fear aging. I don't have to fear loss. While change in this world can bring real grief, there is peace in knowing we have an unchanging identity in Christ.

Because Christ is unchanging, I can know and keep knowing Him. That "sameness" that originally defined identity is fully found in Christ. His invisible attributes, His eternal power and divine nature, Romans tells us, have been clearly perceived since creation. He is the same God of the Old and New Testament. And I get to know Him.

So loved

Remember Carol, back in chapter 2, reading John 3:16 for the very first time? I think some of us need to read it like the very first time again. For God so loved *you* and *me* and *the whole wide world* that He gave His son. There is no better way to describe "so loved" than this. Who you are, and always will be, is so loved.

> But now thus says the LORD, he who created you, O Jacob, he who formed you, O Israel: "Fear not, for I have redeemed you; I have called you by name, you are mine."
>
> Isaiah 43:1

> So that Christ may dwell in your hearts through faith—that you, being rooted and grounded in love, may have strength to comprehend with all the saints what is the breadth and length and height and depth, and to know the love of Christ that surpasses knowledge, that you may be filled with all the fullness of God.
>
> Ephesians 3:17–19

Because I am so loved by Christ, I can love others well. I can love the ungrateful teenager and the sibling who makes sport of controversy. I can keep loving when I'm misunderstood and love some more when I feel empty. I don't have to numb when I feel weary; to know Christ's love is to know that there is always more love.

Because I am so loved by Christ, I don't need to seek that love from the world around me. When I want to be seen, when I want comments, likes, and shares, I must remember I am always seen by Him. I get to show up full, not hungry, not desperate to be filled by the world around me.

Sins forgiven

Because of Christ's finished work on the cross, we live free from the power of sin and death. Again, this is who we are because of what Christ has done.

> If we confess our sins, he is faithful and just to forgive us our sins and to cleanse us from all unrighteousness.
>
> 1 John 1:9

> As far as the east is from the west, so far does he remove our transgressions from us.
>
> Psalm 103:12

Because my sins are forgiven, I don't live in the shame of my past. Any reminder of my past is now an active reminder of what God has saved me from. My story is not a place of guilt but a place of grace, and it glorifies Him.

Because my sins are forgiven, I have good work prepared for me to do. We are saved by grace through faith, Paul says. We are His workmanship created in Christ Jesus for good works.

Inheritance

The word *identity* might not be found in Scripture, but the word *inheritance* is, repeatedly. If we belong to Christ, we have an inheritance, as sons and daughters. We are heirs with Christ. Because of who He is, this is who we are.

> In him we have obtained an inheritance, having been predestined according to the purpose of him who works all things according to the counsel of his will.
>
> Ephesians 1:11

> The Spirit himself bears witness with our spirit that we are children of God, and if children, then heirs—heirs of God and fellow

heirs with Christ, provided we suffer with him in order that we may also be glorified with him.

Romans 8:17

Because I have an inheritance in Christ, I can live with eternity in mind. My inheritance gives perspective to both the struggle and joys of life.

Because I have an inheritance in Christ, I do not strive for approval, but live my numbered days to honor my Father, already approved. I don't have to strive to hustle or impress. I just get serious about faithfully growing fruit in the days He has given me.

Orientation

We've done the heavy lifting. We've trudged deep in the weeds of identity and hopefully come out with a clearer understanding as to how this rootedness in Christ can remind us of what is true and help us to pay attention to that truth even when the world around us is noisy. The next question we need to address is *why?* Why does remembering this really matter? If we know it and believe it, isn't that enough? Does it really matter that we attend to this and keep it in our minds? To answer that, let me tell a little story of directional language.

In the rainforests of New Guinea there is a small people group whose local language is a workhorse. The language is primarily verbal rather than read or written, but that is not what makes it particularly fascinating. It's not *what* they speak, but how much is threaded into the words they speak, that makes the difference.

To communicate more effectively, these people do not simply offer a kind hello or a good-morning smile. Instead, they extend a *"Kametbani!"*—a greeting that not only acknowledges a person's presence or wishes them well, but goes a step further to inform the receiver of the direction the speaker is headed at the moment.

In English, one might roughly translate it "Hello, I'm going up the hill!" The word choice changes slightly depending on the direction the greeter is traveling when the words are exchanged.

Obviously, we could choose to speak this way in English too, but as Michael Wesch notes, "The key difference is not that we *can* say these things. It is that they *have* to. The direction indicator is built right into their grammar, so they have to say which direction they are facing or going every time they say hello."[9] While this is optional in English, it is imbedded, sewn into the local language for these people. Psychologist Lera Boroditsky notes of such languages, "If you don't know which way is which, you literally can't get past hello."[10]

The people of New Guinea aren't the first to use directionally oriented language, but communication bound to spatial orientation has produced some interesting benefits. People who speak such languages "exhibit the uncanny capacity for dead reckoning. They know exactly which direction is which at every moment of the day."[11] Linguist Stephen Levinson tested the fitness of this skill by blindfolding an adult male who speaks Tzeltal, a Mayan language with a similar directional underpinning. Levinson spun the man around more than twenty times in a dark house and he was still able to accurately tell which direction was which. Even young children fluent in directionally oriented languages have shown great adeptness with directions, simply because it is an intrinsic part of their life. To simply acknowledge one another in these parts of the world, you had better know which direction you are going.

Obviously, this is not the case for the English language, as well as most other languages. Direction is optional. Even more, we prize autonomy and the right to anonymity. It's safe to assume we are rather content not informing others about which direction we are heading. But what is interesting is that because we don't rely on the mechanics of a directional language, we are far less inclined to even *know* which direction we are headed.

As believers, there should be no doubt about where we are headed. We are a blood-bought people, so loved, and forgiven with a sure inheritance. This is our identity, and it gives us direction. I wonder if the way we engage in this world, the way we speak to others and process events, the way we work and train our children, the way we travel and plan our days, the way we care for the hurting, spend our money and save it, schedule our time and eat our meals, manage and serve and love and live and give, speaks to the direction we are headed. If we were blindfolded and in a tailspin, by the power of the Holy Spirit, shouldn't we also have an uncanny capacity for dead reckoning? This is what the rootedness of who we are—because of *Whose we are*—can help us remember.

Loss

In addition to our foundational identity in Christ, God has given us many other good and fruitful roles here on earth. He has set us in relationship as daughters and mothers, sisters and cousins or wives, and each of those roles becomes an integral part of not only our good growth, but the good work we are called to do here. He has given us giftings and callings, talents to use in the world that often become part of who we are as well. We get to work heartily as unto the Lord[12] in these capacities, making the best use of our time here. But sometimes, often times, these roles can shift. They can change. And it can rattle who we are.

My grandmother suffered with Alzheimer's the last several years of her life. I say "suffered" because Alzheimer's is a heartbreaking, thieving disease that gradually devours brains cells and thus cognitive ability. For the most part my grandmother endured the burden well. God's mercy was evident. She was mostly happy, but the confusion in her mind did eventually haunt her. The suffering in Alzheimer's is borne also by the family members who must helplessly watch the mind of someone they love gradually slip from reach. As your loved one slowly loses their mind, you slowly seem to lose *them*.

I remember a particular Thanksgiving when my grandmother was in my home for dinner. When the meal was finished, we did as women in my family have done for generations: We began to clear the table and pack up the leftovers. My grandmother was a bit frail, and maneuvering was getting more difficult, so I ushered her into the living room, where she could sit comfortably while we tended to the task at hand. I returned to the dining room table only to find my grandma was following along right behind me. Of course she would be. She had been clearing Thanksgiving tables for longer than I had been alive. She apparently had muscle memory, an orientation to do this work that her mind did not even know. She wasn't about to sit and watch while the rest of us cleared the table. I couldn't help but smile. Hoping to appease her instinct, I handed her a small bowl of olives and asked her to take it to the kitchen for me. She gave me a quiet "yes," but then proceeded to walk right back into the living room and sit quietly with her olives. This is Alzheimer's.

Alzheimer's, I have read, is the world's most common neuro-degenerative disease, with an estimated 20 million cases world-wide. That is 20 million minds slowly losing their grip on the facts and memories of their lives. And perhaps a hundred million more people are watching their mom, their dad, their grandmother mentally fade away. Does this change their value or worth? Does this change how Christ sees the one He loves or the identity, remembered or not, that they have if they have committed their life to Christ? Absolutely not. But the pain of loss of who they were here on earth cannot be ignored.

Perhaps the sting of Alzheimer's has not touched us all, but the decay of this world that shows up in our bodies and our minds, the loss of relationship or loved ones, the change in seasons of parenting or impending retirement is felt abruptly in the way we identify with these good gifts God has given us. It can feel like we are losing part of who we are. This isn't a misplaced identity. As my good friend Maryanne reminded me recently, even Christ, the God of the universe, had functional earthly roles while He was fully man on this earth. He was prophet, priest, and king. In Exodus 31 we read of how God empowered Bezalel and Oholiab by His Spirit with the ability and intelligence, the knowledge and craftsmanship to help construct the tabernacle. God gives roles and empowers good work. We were made for this, and it is natural to feel loss when shifts occur. But this is where our foundational identity in Christ is essential to remember. James says, "He never changes or casts a shifting shadow."[13]

Our work in this world will change. Relationships will change. We will experience times when we feel like we are losing part of who we are. Perhaps that is because we are. We were not made for the transitory, for saying good-bye. We were created for good works and made with hearts fit for eternity. But the Unchanging One meets us here. His Holy Spirit reminds us of truth here, of who we are because of who He is here. We must remember it, friend.

I Am Christian

Joshua Pauling, writing for the *American Reformer*, makes a fair biblical claim to identity in stating that a correct biblical identity is "fully informed by the biblical message and deeply anchored in the historic sacramental practices of the church . . . a *meta-identity* that transcends all others, allowing us to face whatever may come with the same confession of consummate and defini-tive identity made by the ancient martyrs: *Christianus sum.* 'I am Christian.'"[14] Pauling's assessment is a wise one. Although etymology has now taught us that the ancient martyrs would never have called *Chrisitianus sum* their *identity*, his greater point is true. We stand on history, with history, serving the same God. And at the end of the day, every day, we want to be the ones who boldly proclaim in the midst of any and all adversity, gain, or loss, "I am Christian." That is a powerful present truth.

but then she remembered . . .
Whose she is

This is a tricky concept, friend. I warned you we were going to get in some weeds. Let's sort this out a bit more and then get into the Word. Hebrews 11:6 says, "And without faith it is impossible to please him, for whoever would draw near to God must believe that he exists and that he rewards those who seek him." That would make a fine memory verse, wouldn't it? Proceed in faith here, friend. Draw near and seek Him. It honors Him, and He rewards it.

Think about your experience with the term *identity in Christ*. Has the concept been clear or confusing to you? **To the best of your ability, write out a definition of what *identity in Christ* means below.**

Look back to the original definition of *identity* from its Latin root. How does that definition relate to the definition you wrote above?

What about the more modern definitions of *identity* found in this chapter? How do those relate to your definition?

Read 1 Corinthians 15:58. That *therefore* is important. We would be unwise to just dive in here without first figuring out what is going on. Go back and read 1 Corinthians 15:1–4. Paul makes his whole point pretty clear here. **First, what is Paul reminding the church of (v. 1)?**

This is the gospel they are being saved by if they what (v. 2)?

Quick background. The Corinthian church is a bit of mess. The culture in Corinth is highly hedonistic and seems to be influencing the church more than the church is influencing the culture. You see now why Paul is calling them to task here, telling them to hold fast.

In the space below, outline the brief apologetic Paul makes in verses 3–4. He is making four main points. What are they?

Can you think of one word that sums up the points you listed above?

This is what Paul wants the church to remember. So now, we can head back to verse 58.

Therefore (*because of the gospel, because of truth*), he tells them to be _____, _____, always _____ in the work of the Lord, knowing that _____ _____ _____ your labor is not in _____.

What would it look like to abound in the work of the Lord? What work has He given you to abound in?

How does your work, what you are called to do, relate to who you are?

Let's talk about history for a minute. Take a look at Psalm 145:4–7. How is truth passed on?

We have received the story of God's goodness passed down through the ages. If not in our families, then in the faithful among us. This history is a gift.

Read Psalm 61:1–5. What has God given David (v. 5)?

What a blessing! And we know that the fear of the Lord is the beginning of wisdom. We are established with an inheritance because of God's goodness. This is the history that is ours.

If you leave this chapter with more questions than answers on identity, I'm okay with that. We don't need to be scared of questions. But I do want you to *know* and *remember* one thing—Jesus Christ is a firm foundation. Know it and remember, tell it and retell it. This is truth we can hold on to.

Real storms do occur in life. Some will shake us more than others. We may be robbed of jobs we have loved and felt called to. We may grieve over the loss of godly relationships that steadied and supported us here on earth. Grieve well, friend. The loss is real. But so is He.

I have one last Scripture for you. Look up Ephesians 3:14–21; if you have time to take the long route, just read the whole chapter. The mystery of the gospel is mind-blowing. Life-changing. And it is for us because of Him.

I'm praying that we will know this, friend—truly know it and remember it.

5

God's view of time, not ours

Nothing wakes me up to the passage of time like photos. Captures from just four or five short years ago feel like yesterday, but they're not. At all. I know the days are passing, and yet at the same time, it can be startling to observe how quickly it is happening—days slowly sweep into weeks, develop into months, and turn into years right before our eyes. The softness has melted from my kids' faces while time has further pressed itself into my own. And I never even knew it was happening. Time is most tangible in retrospect.

And yet it can be weighty, a struggle, in the present as well. There is potential for much more to be done than the twenty-four hours our days allow. There is *more* we would like to get done, *more* we wish could be done, or more we believe *should* be done. I used to foolishly believe this was a seasonal issue, some seasons of life being naturally more demanding than others. And while this might be partly true, every season of life appears to come with its own time tug-of-war. I recently visited with a few women, each of whom were in their sixties, and in our conversation, every one of them casually alluded to the struggles of time management in their "season" of life. They still work and they watch grand-kids. They serve others and need to maintain and care for their own homes. They are a little more tired than they used to be, and finding the time to do all of these things well is challenging. Of course it is. Why are we so easily tempted to believe that the utopia of time, of balance, is just around the corner in that next stage or season of life? We're fooling ourselves.

The limitations of our time can bring resentment, disillusion-ment, comparison, and shame. *Look at everything she gets done. If only I could get my act together. If only I had more time. If only this work didn't take so much of me . . . or my husband was more helpful . . . or my kids were more . . . (fill in the blank).* I know, because I have at times battled every single one of those thoughts. The limitations of time can feel like a bad round of bumper cars on the midway. We crash into everything around us constantly. There is always something or someone in our way. It's impossible to get anywhere when we are continually distracted by the next demand bumping into us. We get whiplash. But how we view our time is critical here. How we use our time is directly tied to how we move through life in an undistracted manner. And as you'll see later in this chapter, that's exactly the kind of living that Jesus modeled for us.

Time Out

As a homeschooling mom with four kids, I have spent many years believing that meticulous management of our time was the consummate key to our educational success. If I could just get everyone rolling early enough in the morning, and if I could just keep everyone on track until lunch, and then if I could just reel everyone back in, in the afternoon—then we could get it all done successfully.

It wasn't a bad idea in theory, but when you factor in four different learning styles times five different personalities, all of which are bringing five different sets of personal frustrations or struggles to the work they are doing—well, it becomes a math problem with too many variables for any simple formula. Much of the time, things did not move according to *the plan.* But I kept fighting for it.

I remember one specific day when my struggle to rule over our time became very apparent to me. I had sent one of my kids downstairs to practice piano while I finished up a lesson with another child, promising I would be downstairs to hear the progress of the piano player in just a few minutes. When I arrived downstairs, I promptly asked my little piano player to play what he had practiced for me. But he was a wiggly one. He was readying his music, but also shuffling the music on top of the piano. He was scooting himself onto the piano bench, but also being playful about it, flopping this way and that, with a spirited smile on his boyish face. This kid rarely moved from point A to point B in a straight line, and it did not work well for his time-managing mama. So with as much patience as I could muster, I corrected him. "Remember, please don't waste Mommy's time!"

Today was not the first time I had reminded him. I reminded my kids of this quite regularly when they were dawdling or dillydallying or, you know, being kids. *Please don't waste Mommy's time.* The words were familiar to all of us. But this day, however, was the first day I had actually listened to myself. And the full weight of conviction came quickly.

Time was what was to be prized here. My time is what I was instructing my kids to submit to. You, child, are at risk of being a waste of my time; the line is thin and your childishness is bumping right up against it. *Please don't waste my time.* What an ugly message to preach. My time had become my hope for actually doing this job well. My time had become my saving grace. My time was becoming my god. Do you see how easily this happens?

How it began as an idea, a solution, and then a belief? How it became a heart position, a governing ethic that impacted how I thus nurtured and shaped my kids? Idols assert themselves subtly.

You might argue that training our children in expedience is a good thing, and you would be right. Or perhaps that teaching them to be aware of others is courteous. Of course it is. But as Paul Tripp so wisely says, "A desire for a good thing becomes a bad thing when it becomes a ruling thing."[1] My time had become a ruling thing. My time had become an idol.

Have you felt that same struggle with time—perhaps as you are late for an appointment (or even worse, church) and absolutely hot about it. Embarrassment, disappointment, and frustration all become a volatile mix that has you spitting flames. Or maybe it's the hard work of waiting—for your turn, for what you deserve, for what you were promised—that has so consumed your heart and mind, you can't seem to think of anything else. The struggle with time has become a ruling thing.

It's uncomfortable to confront. I know. I easily deserved the *Don't waste my time* bumper sticker. But that is in direct opposition to what we have been called to as followers of Christ. Thankfully, in His Word, God has graciously given us some excellent examples to remember when it comes to time. Remembering the path Christ has modeled for us here is key to living out our beliefs in earnest, to paying full attention to what really matters and not getting lost in distraction in the process.

Interruption vs. Distraction

The humanity of Jesus Christ is an indispensable gift to us as believers. Every challenge we face, He met and mastered. And many of them have been recorded in His Word as a guide for us. The Bible doesn't speak of endless notifications, group texts, and strings of emails, but it does speak of people with real needs showing up in Christ's path *constantly*. Wherever He went, crowds followed with needs and questions and frustrations and problems. He entered a city, and people came running. He got in a boat to cross to the other side of the sea, and people would race to meet Him there. Can you even imagine? So many people with all kinds of mixed motives wanting so many things, constantly. And his most common response? *He was moved with compassion.* Over and over again, He stopped what He was doing, paused from the task at hand, and tended to the needy hearts right in front of Him.

That's a message, isn't it, friend? Jesus addressed the needs in front of Him. People were never an interruption from the *real* work of ministry; they *were* the real ministry. Jesus was never once distracted from His greater mission, but He was also not frustrated by the obvious interruptions. He understood the difference between distraction and interruption quite well. And He knew His job there.

Interestingly enough, it seems we were actually created to thrive in similarly interrupted environments. In 1927, Russian psychologist Dr. Bluma Zeigarnik studied the impact of interruption on task-related memory and completion. Dr. Zeigarnik was fascinated as she watched a busy waitstaff memorize multiple orders while tending busy tables. She observed that the mental recall of the staff was far better on open orders, but declined drastically once an order was completed. Further research uncovered the fact that interruptions create cognitive tension that actually empowers us to not only complete the task after the interruption, but better remember it as well. In psychology circles, this is known as the Zeigarnik effect, and the research behind it is the reason that your favorite show or book leaves you on a cliffhanger. They know that cognitive tension heightens attention and will keep you coming back. It's the reason you're tempted to binge the whole season in one sitting; this hunger for completion, to know, increases not only our likelihood of completing the task, but our short-term memory of it as well. Not only is this good news for all of us frequently frustrated by the seemingly endless interruptions of our lives, but it's good news because it evidences how we are divinely fitted for the good work we are called to do as interrupted women.

Interruptions do not equal distractions. Unless you live in a hobbit hole, interruptions are likely part of the work you are called to do as a leader, a mother, a daughter, a friend who loves and serves people with real needs that don't always fit tidily into your schedule. We are fitted to handle interruptions quite well as we run the race set before us. Remember, we are fearfully and wonderfully made, friend!

Most of the time we get it backward. We are more than willing to entertain our distractions, while frequently annoyed by life's interruptions. Distractions impact our sense of mission, while interruptions impact our sense of moment. Are we willing to concede our present moments for our greater mission, or do we continually subvert our greater mission for our desire in the moment? It's not a fair trade. Let's follow Jesus's lead in the moment and the mission.

Moment vs. Mission

We might be tempted to think that Jesus didn't really care about time. I mean, He was fully God, right? Maybe He could joyfully tend to every interruption because time just wasn't something He needed to concern himself with. But Scripture tells us otherwise. Jesus made reference to time repeatedly, and each reference shows His care for a greater concept of time—not merely tied to the moment, but to the greater mission. At Jacob's well, in a discourse with the Samaritan woman, Jesus assured her, "But the hour is coming, and is now here, when the true worshipers will worship the Father in spirit and truth."[2] Jesus was revealing himself as the very fulfillment of the law here. All of biblical history was pointing toward this moment, the fullness of time,[3] Paul called it. This was Jesus's time, and He was fully aware of it.

A few chapters earlier, when the wine ran dry at the wedding in Cana, Jesus's mother wanted to make sure Jesus understood the problem. "They have no wine," she said, with the hope and expectation of a mother who knows exactly what her son is capable of. "Woman, what does this have to do with me? My hour has not yet come."[4] His response to His own mother was His keen sense of the Father's timing.

And of course in the garden of Gethsemane, with His closest followers—who failed to keep themselves awake long enough to pray with Him—Jesus pleaded, "So, could you not watch with me one hour? Watch and pray that you may not enter into temptation. The spirit indeed is willing, but the flesh is weak."[5] His gentleness toward their failure, their lack of urgency in His great moment of need, is beautiful, isn't it? Christ's compassion for and intimate knowledge of the frame of those who love Him is a mercy that reverberates. This was another failed attempt for them, and the timing was not lost on him. "See, the hour is at hand, and the Son of Man is betrayed into the hands of sinners."[6]

Yes, Jesus understood timing. Perhaps even a sense of urgency, one could say. But it never came at the expense of deeply loving those who were right in front of Him. His wholehearted devotion to the greater mission never compromised or eclipsed His ability to love deeply in the moment. He was interruptible but never distracted. What a beautiful challenge for us. We must possess a sense of the Father's time. We must stay focused on our mission. And we mustn't overlook the immense opportunity of the moment.

Denying a Scarcity Mindset

The limited nature of time can develop an ache in us if we're not careful. It can feel bossy. A few nights ago I spent Valentine's evening home with my husband and kids. We overdid it in the best way, celebrating a sweet evening with grilled steaks and baby potatoes, a house favorite Caesar salad, homemade rosemary focaccia, and a caramel butter cake with fudge filling. And chocolate-covered strawberries. It was a lovely feast. I went to bed that evening counting time backward. You know that strategy, right? I wondered, *What if this is the last Valentine's dinner I get with all six of us gathered around the table together?* I have teens that are charging toward adulthood, and there are just no guarantees we'll even get to do this again. Ever. Even beautiful moments in time can be lined with scarcity, bruised with perceived lack.

I love the way Jesus met the woman at the well in Samaria. He was feeling His humanity. John tells us He was weary—tired or worn, some translations say—from his journey. He had left Judea, was headed north to Galilee, and wasn't afraid to take the less popular route straight through Samaria. He parked himself beside Jacob's well. Can you imagine? Exhausted from a long and dusty day of travel, and finally resting, finding a bit of solace propped up against the well while His disciples continued into town to find some food. We know this kind of tired, don't we? It feels familiar.

Jesus meets the Samaritan woman there. She shows up right in the midst of His tiring journey, and after He asks for a drink, she engages Him in conversation. And He says, "I'm weary. Please don't waste my time."

No, no, He doesn't. The interruption of His rest doesn't even phase Him; His weariness or limited energy isn't even a thought, because this conversation right here is the very thing He lives for—to share truth, to speak hope, to save the world. It isn't only His calling or His goal, it is his sustenance. Later, when the disciples return with the food they had purchased, they urge Him to eat. But He said to them, "I have food to eat that you do not know about." The disciples, their eyes on the earthly just like ours so often are, start wondering who slipped Jesus some food. But Jesus guides them further. "My food is to do the will of him who sent me and to accomplish his work."[7] *That* is a sense of mission, friend.

Jesus was fully man, remember. He hungered; He ate. But He also knew the only place He could be truly filled and fed, satisfied and sustained. He did not operate from a scarcity mindset, prioritizing His physical needs out of what would have seemed like legitimate concern that there might not be time or space or supply later. No, Jesus Christ was living out the Sermon on the Mount, which He preached to these very disciples:

> "Therefore I tell you, do not be anxious about your life, what you will eat or what you will drink, nor about your body, what you will put on. Is not life more than food, and the body more than clothing? Look at the birds of the air: they neither sow nor reap nor gather into barns, and yet your heavenly Father feeds them. Are you not of more value than they? And which of you by being anxious can add a single hour to his span of life?"[8]

Our scarcity mindset is a lie. We need not live from lack, counting backward with the prevailing feeling that there is never quite enough time. We instead live numbering our days,[9] not for fear of them running out, but for wisdom to value them as precious and to live them well.

That Samaritan woman went and told her whole town about the man who told her everything she ever did. The townspeople came and saw the Savior of the world, and many believed, all because of that first interruption, because Jesus trusted His Father with every lack humanity afforded Him.

Jesus soon departed, back on His way to Galilee. Filled. Full. Never once distracted from where He was headed. This is our model.

Jesus Was After His Father's Heart

In their book *Made to Stick,* Chip Heath and Dan Heath share a fascinating story of strategic planning within the United States Army. They detail the chain of command from the president to the Joint Chiefs of Staff and so on down the line that outlines specific objectives, plans, and orders, which flows further down to generals, colonels, and captains. According to Heath, "The orders snowball until they accumulate enough specificity to guide the actions of individual foot soldiers at particular moments in time."[10] That is pretty specific and detailed planning.

The trouble is, as the Heath brothers acknowledge, the plans often turn out to be useless. They fail frequently. Why? Because unpredictable and unexpected things happen. You can't always guess how the enemy will respond, and that can be a game changer. Leading with such narrow specificity causes the leadership to create a plan that could be useless almost immediately. The variables are too great, the individual responses required too numerous to make a plan of specific individual action that will stick.

In response to this struggle, in the 1980s, the army developed an updated method called Commander's Intent (CI), where intentions and end goals were outlined in a very clear directive at the top of each order. According to Colonel Tom Kolditz at West Point in response to this change, "You can lose the ability to execute the original plan, but you never lose the responsibility of executing intent."[11] The Heath brothers weren't writing a book to promote the gospel, but I'm not sure there is a better analogy for us as believers trying to give God our full attention in a highly distracted world. We can attempt well-laid plans to read the Bible in a year, to serve our church, and practice hospitality with flourish this year. But maybe sickness shakes our family for a season. The people right in front of us might face challenges that demand our love and support in ways we never expected, and that may mess up our plans to serve at church or open our home. We get behind on the Bible reading schedule again and are tempted to toss the entire plan for the year. But our primary goal must be to follow Christ and imitate Him. We might lose our ability to execute our original plan, but we never lose the responsibility of executing intent.

Jesus spoke of this frequently in the book of John, telling us that He speaks of what He has seen with His father, that He honors His Father, He received authority from His Father, and that He and the Father are one, to name only a few. Jesus was *always* following the heart of the Father, the Commander's Intent. Our goal and our desire should be the same. It's popular right now to talk about the nuances of Scripture, and I remember as a young believer thinking it would be far easier if God would have just given us a detailed list of do's and don'ts, a la 1970s United States Army. I'm tempted to think I'd like a specific plan of action for every foot soldier on the ground in every situation. Except, that ultimately wasn't effective, was it?

Our Father has done one better than an updated method of relaying orders. He has gifted us with the Holy Spirit helper to teach us all things and to bring to remembrance all the things He has spoken to us through His Word. He engages us through relationship rather than only rules. We are to follow His heart, His command, His intent, but we are never alone in our quest for obedience. We might be a culture of good forgetters, but we have a Holy Spirit helper to remind us who God is, how He works, and how He loves.

New Neighbors

One of the most familiar stories in all of Scripture has to be the parable of the Good Samaritan. It has been told and retold in familiarity, almost like a fable. Except it's actually straight from Scripture. But that telling and retelling can sometimes wear the story out a bit. If familiarity doesn't breed contempt, at the very least it muddies the details.

Take the alphabet, from the perspective of a wise and clever four-year-old. They know it. They can nail the song. And they have no idea what *elemenopee* is. They just sing it solid, inviting us to sing it with them next time. And the details are still likely lost on them. As adults, we do that in more grown-up ways, particularly when it comes to Bible stories we have known since we ourselves were four years old.

Let's take the time to trek through the story of the Good Samaritan[12] a little more slowly. The story is a parable, yes. It's a story with a purpose, used to make a point. It's basically what I'm doing in this book right now. (Just copying Jesus, friend!) But this story is told in response to a question that we almost always forget in our recall of the parable. A lawyer with ill intent attempts to put Christ to the test by cornering him with a question. "Teacher, what shall I do to inherit eternal life?" The scribe is here to be taught, but in his pride, he thinks he will teach Jesus a lesson.

Even if his intent is less than virtuous, his question is a good one, and Jesus responds, "What is written in the Law? How do you read it?" Jesus answers the question in kind, wisely putting the onus back on the lawyer, who should indeed be well versed in the law. He engages in conversation, as we see Him do so often in Scripture. The attorney answers with the expertise his occupation would afford him: "You shall love the Lord your God with all of your heart and with all your soul and with all your strength and with all your mind, and your neighbor as yourself." Quoting Jesus's own words of the great commandment, the lawyer nails it, and Jesus tells him so.

But the scribe doesn't stop there. He pushes further, desiring self-justification, Scripture tells us. "And who is my neighbor?" the lawyer bites back. This is the question that initiates the parable of the Good Samaritan. We can make the story about all kinds of things, we can point out lessons and morals worth noting, but Jesus told the parable as an answer to a specific question: "Who is my neighbor?"

So Jesus brings the story in response. A man was traveling from Jerusalem to Jericho one day and robbers attacked him. They beat him, stripped him, and left him for dead. Now, most Scripture translations say "by chance" a priest was walking down the road, and when he saw the beaten man lying there, he passed by on the other side. He wanted nothing to do with him. Perhaps he was thinking, *Don't waste my time.* Next up a Levite comes along and passes the beaten man just as the priest did. But alas, a Samaritan man comes along. Luke says, "But a Samaritan, as he journeyed, came to where he was, and when he saw him, he had compassion. He went to him and bound up his wounds, pouring on oil and wine." When he finishes the story, Jesus asks the lawyer one more question: "Which of these three, do you think, proved to be a neighbor to the man who fell among the robbers?" The lawyer responds, "The one who showed him mercy." And Jesus said to him, "You go, and do likewise."

There are a couple important things to unpack here. First, the whole Samaritan thing—it's familiar and yet foreign to us, so let's remember what is at play. There is a major long-standing rift between the Jews and the Samaritans. Back when the Assyrians invaded Israel from the north in 721 BC, they took the Israelites captive. Some of the Jewish people chose to marry Assyrians, making their families half Jewish and half Gentile. When they returned to Israel some seventy years later, these people settled together in Samaria. Mixing cultures, they practiced a few different customs and chose to worship God on Mount Gerazim rather than in the temple in Jerusalem. And the rift only grew. The Jewish people and the Samaritans strictly avoided one another.

But God. Earlier we discussed Jesus engaging the Samaritan woman at the well in John 4, offering her eternal life, and in turn much of her community chose to follow Christ that day.

And here we see Jesus making the point that your neighbor is perhaps not who you would have ever thought it would be. Of all the people who came across the beaten Jewish man that day, *his people* didn't want to be bothered with him, didn't want to be interrupted by his needs. But the Samaritan man? He saw the Jewish man. That was his first move, simply to *see* him. And then he was moved with compassion. He refused to distract himself elsewhere, to cross to the other side of the street and look away. He saw and moved toward that man in compassion. And finally, in mercy, he attended to his needs. Jesus is showing us how to be a neighbor. Let's pay attention.

One last detail I find interesting in this parable is the mention that the Samaritan found the beaten man "on his journey," the CSB version says. I wonder where the Samaritan was going that day. Where was he journeying to? Scripture doesn't tell us, so we don't need to know, but we don't get the sense that he was on a mission to find a beaten Jewish man on the side of the road. He was going about his business, whatever and wherever that might be. And the person God put in his path? That was his neighbor that day.

Here's the thing: We frequently forget who our neighbors are. We look long and high, follow by way of rabbit trail an incredibly moving story of a pediatric transplant patient halfway around the world, and we're moved by it. We want to help them. And that is beautiful. We can thank God for the connective beauty of the internet by which we get to help people all over the world. But God often puts neighbors directly in our path. They are the little people you get to wake up and serve each day. They are the people at the office who are a little hard to love some days. They are your in-laws and the man you pledged to do life with. Those are the neighbors God has placed right in front of you. Sometimes it's easier to look around the world for neighbors. But God has given us people to see, be moved with His compassion toward, and show His mercy to, right in front of us every single day. Let's refuse to miss the opportunity, to miss them. Let's love like Christ—always interruptible, never distracted, always on mission for his glory.

We can either move away or we can be moved with compassion. Let's be moved with compassion.

Our time must be submitted to Christ. He can and will remind us of the Father's heart and our eternal mission here. If only we will ask; if only we will remember.

but then she remembered . . . God's view of time

Let's talk about time. Time management is a hot topic in our world. It sells books, courses, planners, apps, you name it. An entire industry stands ready to solve our time-management issues, but do we ever really make progress? I mean, authors are still writing and selling books on the topic. I hope you paused at Paul Tripp's words in this chapter: "A desire for a good thing becomes a bad thing when it becomes a ruling thing." That is a powerful reminder on all sorts of fronts. The application is broad. It's often the "good" things in our life that, unattended, become idols. Do a quick self-assessment on your relationship with time. Are you generous with it? Weighed down by it? Stingy with it? Overwhelmed by it? Saddened by it? Mostly unaware of it? Be honest.

Let's take a look at some words from Solomon, who is credited with being an incredibly wise man. **First read 1 Kings 4:29–34 for a little background on Solomon. What can you learn about his explicit wisdom here?**

Who gave it to him?

How did it compare to others?

What are some things he was wise about?

(For the fascinating story on Solomon's request for knowledge, read 1 Kings 3.)

Now read Ecclesiastes 3:1–8. This is a beautifully poetic piece written by Solomon, that man of wisdom and understanding we just read about. Ecclesiastes 3:1 both introduces and sums up the poem. **Write that first verse out in the space below.**

What would you say was Solomon's perspective on time? How does that relate to what you said your relationship is with time, in the first question?

One of our greatest challenges with time is to see it from God's perspective. Matthew Henry sums up Solomon's words by saying, "All our pains and care will not alter either the mutable nature of the things themselves or the immutable counsel of God concerning them."[13] *Mutable* means changing, and *immutable* means unchanging, if those words are tripping you up. So what he is saying is all of our fretting and worrying will never change the fact that things change, or the fact that God is the unchanging ruler over them all. What a beautiful truth! Similar to the question we asked earlier: What am I believing to be true about God here? We can ask a similar, more specific question when change and time feel desperate—am I remembering that God is unchanging here?

Let's dig a little deeper into the concept of distractions vs. interruptions. Remember through the life of Christ we see that He was very interruptible and yet never distracted. He always had the greater purpose, His Father's purpose, in mind. However, it is actually more common for us to be frustrated by interruptions and quietly give way to the distractions. **Why do you think that might be?**

In your Bible turn to Luke 2:41 and read on to verse 52.
How old was Jesus in this passage (v. 42)?
How long was He missing (v. 46)?
What was He doing and how did those around Him respond? (v. 46)?

Can you even imagine? Jesus was fully man—or fully boy at this point. And his parents were fully human. So every ache of losing your child for three whole days is real. If you are a parent, or have had an opportunity to care for a child, have you ever misplaced a child? I couldn't find my three-year-old daughter for thirty whole seconds at Disneyland once. I might be exaggerating; it may have been fifteen seconds. But it was just long enough to feel my heart crashing through my chest, to think, *I don't care how big this place is, I will search every ride and restaurant like an absolute maniac until I find her.* I didn't have to search any rides or restaurants, thankfully. She was just down the way, happily walking along with another family she thought was her own. Anyhow, I *feel* for Mary here. But that's not really the point. **Write the twelve-year-old Jesus's response to his parents below (v. 49).**

I love the way the New King James Version puts this verse: "Why did you seek Me? Did you not know that I must be about my Father's business?"[14] This was Jesus's response to His parents, but it was also the response of His *entire life*. Amidst every interruption, every temptation, every opportunity for distraction, He was about His Father's business. This must be our goal too. It reshapes and reframes the way we view our time.

Try something a little silly with me, just for fun. Spell your full name *without* using the letters L-M-N-O-P. What would your name be? (If your name is bereft of these letters, try it with the name of a spouse or a friend.)

These five letters stuck in the middle of the alphabet and pronounced by the average four-year-old—and a few of us older alphabet singers—as "elemenopee" are quite important, aren't they? Most names and many words just won't work without them. We get something different entirely. It's a simple illustration, but it is an important one. When we come to Scripture with familiarity that glosses over the details, we can fail to see something really important. Something God put there on purpose. So let's look closer at the very familiar story of the Good Samaritan in Luke 10.

Jesus tells this parable in response to what question?

Who is asking the question, and why?

What do we know about his intent?

If you have kids, or have been around kids, or have ever in your life been a kid, you know that *intention* matters. For kids and adults. But Jesus, ever about His father's business, takes the opportunity to teach the lawyer and everyone else in earshot, and us. How does the lawyer answer Jesus's question "Which of these three, do you think, proved to be a neighbor to the man who fell among the robbers?" (v. 37).

And what does Jesus command that lawyer (and us) in verse 37?

This is our job, friend. We don't need to go looking for neighbors; we only need to see the ones God has already put in front of us. We need the help of the Holy Spirit to see them, to be moved with compassion for them, and to attend to their needs. Pause and pray that He would help you do just that. I have to believe that is a prayer that the Father loves to answer.

Further study: I thought you might like to take a look at some famous artists' renditions of the familiar parable we read about today. There are so many of them; a few of my favorites are by Willian Henry Margetson, Rembrandt, and Maximilien Luce. You can find links to these on my website www.katiewestenberg.com, or simply enter the artist's name into your internet search engine and "The Good Samaritan," and their works should be easy for you to find.

6

say so

why telling the story matters

The Bible is incredibly repetitive. It's full of history, poetry, prophecy, and the most unbelievably true love story, but it's also really repetitive. The Old Testament is sewn deeply into the New Testament, threaded throughout, and quoted repeatedly. Stories of God's faithfulness are told and retold and retold again. The gospels detail similar stories and events in the life of Christ, giving the reader a robust view from varied angles, but also simply reminding us of the story over and over again. For example, Luke tells the story of Paul's conversion three times in the book of Acts alone.[1]

I think it is safe to assume the Holy Spirit knew our feeble minds would need repetition for understanding. I think He knew we'd be good forgetters. It is the nature of our Father to meet us in the reality of our humanity and to parent us with the wisdom of our present frame. This is how a compassionate Father loves the children who so desperately need His help, who consistently struggle to remember truth, to remember who He is and how He loves. He tells them. He shows them. And He does it again and again. The repetition of Scripture is for our good. This is love.

We discussed earlier how in the book of Philippians, Paul tells the church, "Finally my brothers, rejoice in the Lord. To write the same things to you is no trouble to me and is safe for you."[2] The New Living Translation words that last sentence, "I never get tired of telling you these things and I do it to safeguard your faith." He goes on to talk about the good work of living for Christ—about counting everything else as loss but knowing Christ, about pressing on toward the prize for which we are called, about standing firm and rejoicing in the Lord. Paul's exhortation here, while of great value, isn't the point I want you to notice as much as his preface. He's telling the church that he acknowledges he has already told them this stuff.

We see Peter doing the same thing when he says, "I think it right, as long as I am in this body, to stir you up by way of reminder"[3] and Jude as well when he tells the church, "Now I want to remind you, although you once fully knew it, that Jesus, who saved a people out of the land of Egypt, afterward destroyed those who did not believe."[4] Do you notice the theme in what the Holy Spirit has encouraged these men to write? They were reminding these believers of what they should know, what they once knew. To protect them. To love them. Repetition is for our good and for God's glory.

Do It Again

What was your favorite book when you were a child? How many times did you read it? Were you obsessed with it for a short season or for years? Mine was *We Help Mommy*. I loved it for years; I'm still not quite over it! Just thinking of it brings nostalgia—happy remembering. It was a Little Golden Book about a brother and sister who helped their mommy with house chores. Perhaps it was propaganda, but I absolutely loved that book. I loved it when the little girl got to wash her doll clothes with the laundry and hang them out to dry. I loved when she got to help with the grocery shopping and when she used cherries and pie crust to make a treat for her daddy. I loved that she only had one brother just like me. My mom read *We Help Mommy*, and I later read it to myself until the back cover fell off and the last page had to be taped. And I kept on reading it. I still have it, in its so-well-loved-it-is-barely-held-together state. If you have had children or have been around children, or perhaps remember once being a child, you know that children often attach themselves to a book, at least for a season, and love to read it again and again without tiring.

G. K. Chesterton cracks open the point I'm trying to make here:

> Because children have abounding vitality, because they are in spirit fierce and free, therefore they want things repeated and unchanged. They always say, "Do it again"; and the grown-up person does it again until he is nearly dead. For grown-up people are not strong enough to exult in monotony. But perhaps God is strong enough to exult in monotony. It is possible that God says every morning, "Do it again" to the sun; and every evening, "Do it again" to the moon."[5]

That is worth considering, friend. Perhaps God is strong enough to exult in monotony. Perhaps He wrote repetition into our world and into his Word not simply because He knows the extent of our weak frame, our dull minds, but for love, because He glories, He rejoices in uniformity even as He does creativity. Because repetition too is a gift.

We use the word *monotony* as if it were something negative. According to its etymology, the word's originally transferred definition in 1706 meant "wearisome sameness" and "tiresome uniformity."[6] But I wonder if we have laid more subjective adjectives upon the word than it was intended to bear. The consistency of an inhale and exhale could be *profound* sameness, couldn't it? The uniformity of a dahlia's petals or a newborn's heartbeat could be *wondrous* uniformity, could it not? Chesterton wisely points out that children have a proclivity toward monotony, which we seem to lose in maturity. All of our worldly wisdom leaves us repulsed by sameness, bored by it, or at the very least, neglectful of it. But what if faith like a child includes at least some of the wonder and hunger of childhood as well? What if the kingdom of heaven belongs to such as these who can glory in repetition, in the unrelenting beauty of His reminders, His sameness, that really is beauty itself. Romans 1 tells us that God's invisible attributes—His eternal power and divine nature—are made evident throughout creation, so we are without excuse. I think sunrises and sunsets, as Chesterton suggests, just might qualify. These are things made that speak of God's very nature. They are daily reminders of His character. Far greater than a little red dot on your app, God fires up the sky with the greatest notification we could possibly receive. *Pay attention to this. It points to me.*

Same Old Story

My dad has an uncle and a cousin who are among his best friends, but they don't get to see each other often. They are separated by many miles, but they talk on the phone with each other faithfully. Mostly, when they speak, they rehash old stories. They are all roughly the same age and spent their childhood together hunting and fishing and doing all the things young boys and men did in those days. They built a deep store of memories together and they love nothing better than digging deep into that storehouse during their phone conversations and retrieving a favorite memory say so • 121

to retell and relive. Any one of them will add to the story as it is resurrected yet again, and every one of them will end up laughing so hard that tears will often come.

My mom thinks it's a little silly. "I don't know how they do it," she'll say. "They tell those same old stories time after time and they never tire of them. They seem to only laugh harder each time." My mom is right, it does seem a little silly. Childlike, almost. But I'm beginning to wonder if that is the key. They aren't *just* rehashing old stories; they are remembering a relationship that continues to strengthen in the retelling. Like an oral tradition that cultures have passed down for generations, the stories my dad and his family share are part history and part entertainment. They don't defy monotony; they exult in it and nurture connection in the meantime. My dad and his family are sharing a history that is building with time, not because they get to see each other but because they aren't afraid to enjoy repetition. This is part of how they love each other.

I want to stop circling and get to the point here. We are called to become monotonous storytellers, but we must understand that this *is* beauty. This is both how He loves and how we love. We are called to be rememberers and relentless sharers of truth. We hear the psalmists proclaim this repeatedly:

I will sing of the steadfast love of the LORD, forever; with my mouth I will make known your faithfulness to all generations.

Psalm 89:1

Sing to the LORD, bless his name; tell of his salvation from day to day. Declare his glory among the nations, his marvelous works among all the peoples!

Psalm 96:2–3

Oh give thanks to the LORD; call upon his name; make known his deeds among the peoples! Sing to him, sing praises to him;

tell of all his wondrous works! Glory in his holy name; let the hearts of those who seek the LORD rejoice!

Psalm 105:1–3

Let the Redeemed of the LORD say so, whom he has redeemed from trouble.

Psalm 107:2

Can you see it? With our words, our song, we get to make known the *faithfulness of God* to future generations. We give our full attention to God in the retelling, and sear that truth even deeper in our souls as we do. We aren't just sharing stories of the good old days, or passing on oral tradition, each of which have their place, no doubt. But we get to declare God's glory, His salvation from day to day to the world around us. We get to make His deeds known as we give thanks and call upon His name. He has redeemed us from sin and death, friend, the wrath we deserve. We are the redeemed and it is both our job and our joy to say so. *We must be the ones who say so.* Remembering is more than a mental act. It's step one in passing down the faith we ourselves cling to today, and when we commit to this act, we are doing our part to keep the next generation of eyes fixed on Jesus while we steady our gaze on Him as well. If we don't, who will?

I love how Psalm 96 even mentions the frequency of this work—we are to tell of our salvation *day to day*. Matthew Henry says, "Let day unto day utter this speech, that, under the influence of gospel devotions, we may daily exemplify a gospel conversation."[7] We often make "saying so" harder than it needs to be. We make it about a platform or prepared speech, a sermon. We put more complex words to it, evangelism, and ministry. But "day to day" brings an earthy practicality to it, a beautiful monotony perhaps. We are under the influence of gospel devotion. What if we just got more serious about having regular gospel conversations?

Henry's word choice is also helpful. As we live devoted to the gospel, we ought to make it our goal to "exemplify" a gospel conversation, which alludes to more than our spoken words and also to the actions and interactions of our lives. How we choose to live is all part of our gospel conversation. As we grow in becoming people attentive to Christ, focusing not on what is seen but on what is eternal, fully aware that we are the redeemed, we should be people who *live* a gospel conversation. The gospel is our life. Rod Dreher expounds on this idea: "The way Christians talk about God and weave the stories of the Bible and church history into the fabric of domestic life is of immense significance, precisely because these things are so ordinary."[8] Our ordinary is fertile soil for passing on our faith. We simply need to say so.

We can be the redeemed who say so in how we relate to the store clerk and mail carrier. We can say so in the way we tend to the never-ending tasks of cleaning toilets or serving the needy inside our homes and beyond. We can let the truth of God's Word reform our lives and our words so that it becomes part of every conversation, every decision. This should be the way we respond and the way we repent when our responses aren't righteous. This should be the way we forgive. The way we love. This is what it means to live a gospel conversation day to day, friend.

In committing our lives to saying so daily, a couple things happen. First, we strengthen the foundations. Looking to testify to the goodness of God inherently means we will find it. We will remember Him as the source and hope of our salvation. We will be reminded of who He is and how He loves through His Word. We will be reminded of His goodness through the lived "saying so" of other believers. Remember, this is who He is. If we are looking, we will see it.

Sharing the goodness of God strengthens our remembrance. It roots that truth even deeper in us before it ever blesses anyone else. This is the story of my dad and his uncle and cousin. They *want* to dig up a good old story. They search that storehouse, and they find. They rehash and they remember even better, with even greater joy perhaps. The act of digging and reliving strengthens their connection to one another. They aren't only reminded of a good story, they aren't only able to share a good laugh, they are reminded that this relationship matters, that it is valued, that it has deep and important roots. They are strengthening the foundations. That is what remembering does.

Our good growth in saying so is not predicated upon our present circumstances. This is vital. As modern people, we have come to idolize the moment. Social media is fueled by it. The value of the moment, of now, is everything, because it keeps you coming back, keeps you scrolling, keeps you refreshing. There is always new content, new fodder, new news, now, and now, and now. The nature of the beast cannot help but make us circumstantially oriented people, because the feed is always dominated by the now. We are trained to prize the present. But the present is unpredictable, for believers and unbelievers alike. No matter what our current circumstances are, in plenty or in want, saying so—weaving that truth of who God is and how He loves into our minds—helps us stake our claim in unsettling seas.

Golden Retrieval

From the science side of things, there are two basic keys to memory—encoding and retrieval. Encoding is the formation of a memory, and retrieval is, as you might assume, the recall of it. While encoding processes often gain most of the attention in memory studies (think about how we put information in our brains), more recent research has shown that retrieval has been grossly neglected.

According to a report by the American Psychological Association, "Practicing retrieval has been shown to produce more learning than engaging in other effective encoding techniques."[9] Did you catch that? The hinge pin really moving our memories to long-term storage is retrieval. It's not manipulating how we get the information *in* that is making a huge difference; it is getting the information *out*, over and over again, that makes it stick. It's learning and then telling, and then telling again. It's saying so. It's almost like God designed this whole process to work as He intended it to, isn't it? Like He fashioned us for obedience, to know His Word, His commands, and follow them. Of course He did, friend. Of course He did.

According to that same report, "Many students view retrieval as a 'knowledge check'; they test themselves to see if they know something, rather than out of the belief that practicing retrieval itself will help them learn." This is our learning habit. We are all tempted to be this kind of student. We know it, so we think we'll always know it. We can find Scripture monotonous, skipping over the verses we already know, because we already know them. But this familiarity is learning. Retrieval and recall are further, deeper learning. God tells us to tell and retell not only for the good of those around us (yes, of course!), but for our good as well. We get to drill truth because we need it. Long term. Say so.

Truth Spreaders

Weaving the Bible and church history into the very fabric of our domestic lives becomes the simplest way for us to spread truth. This is where we practice the retrieval that grows the listener and grows us. We don't have to search for opportunities: they are daily. We simply need to take advantage of them. The science of habit formation says we must tie our desired habit to rituals that already exist, as doing so provides a natural cue for our new habit. Domestic life is a pretty solid cue. Could we weave a gospel conversation into our dinnertime routine? Could we turn down the radio and find space for gospel conversations while we commute in the car? Could we intentionally say so as we work side by side in the garden?

My kids love for my husband and I to tell stories of our childhood over and over again. They usually ask for the ones when we were naughty and got in trouble because they think they're funny. I'm not saying every conversation has to flow like a Sunday school lesson. That would be failure because this isn't Sunday school, this is life. But the stories we tell and the exchanges we have, the way we process bad news with a friend or sit with a child who is scared, the way we process discipline or walk through forgiveness, must be shaped by the goodness of God because our lives are shaped by the goodness of God. Gospel conversations are necessarily what must pour out of a heart transformed by the gospel. We have the opportunity to pass on truth in the simple domesticity of our everyday lives. And if we don't choose to thoughtfully do so, what story then will our lives tell?

In our home, this looks like a hard stop after breakfast, which we call "morning meeting," a time when we all gather and discuss the day ahead. Don't picture a formal setting; that is not what it is, at least for us. One child might be stepping away from math books while another is fresh out of the shower. The youngest might be rolled up like a blanket burrito on the floor, and it is quite likely that one or more of us will be irritated about who is sitting where. This is our domestic life. We read Scripture and often work on memorization together or read a devotional. We take time to pray together. I often will share with the kids what I noticed in my personal Bible reading that morning, or we will discuss a current news event and try to think through it biblically.

This is one way we make space, fixed rhythms, for gospel conversations. But so much of the Spirit's best work is done in lesser scheduled moments of life. When overwhelm surfaces in the life of my friends, or my kids, or me, I have been gifted the opportunity of gospel conversations. When frustration or fear about politics or relationships, finances or education, looms heavy in the hearts of those I love, it becomes an invitation for a gospel conversation. Together we can quiet the desperate distraction and be reminded that we don't do this work in our might or power, but by His Spirit. Being aware of unexpected moments for these types of conversations allows us to strengthen our memory in the retrieval of truth, declare God's goodness in the retelling of it, and honor Him as we guide our attention away from our circumstances and back to Him.

Story Told

I went to a funeral recently of a woman I didn't know very well. I knew her, just not well. She was more of an acquaintance. Her name was Deena, and we went to church together but never actually sat in the same pew. We attended the same Sunday school class for a while, but it is a class for listening more than talking, so I can't say that I ever really got to know Deena there. I did taste her incredible chocolate earthquake cake once, and I still have the copy of the recipe she gave me. My husband knows Deena's husband. We know her kids a little more. She had a kind and generous smile. But that is about all I knew of her before attending her funeral.

Deena's service was traditional, with several friends and family members sharing memories from years of knowing Deena. I learned that she loved to sew and was quite proficient at it. She loved to cook, and people loved to eat her food. She loved teaching and taught for forty-two years at the same school, and she loved being outdoors with her family, hiking and camping, while raising her three kids. But what caught my attention was how every single person spoke of Deena's faithfulness. They spoke repeatedly of her love for Jesus and her love for others. I didn't know Deena well, but this is the story she lived, and this is the story her life told. This is how she is going to be remembered.

As I looked around the sanctuary during her funeral, so many faces, most of whom I didn't know, I couldn't help but think, *Every single one of us is going to do this. Every person in these pews is going to have a funeral eventually.* The story of our lives and our loves and how we navigated our days is going to be told by someone else. We may say a few profound words in our lives, we may write a few powerful sentences, but the message we live repeatedly day in, day out, is the one that will be told and remembered. Deena's story was simple and consistent, and honorable. She told it in days and weeks and years. She lived it with days numbered, wisely.[10] And the remembering is only a further blessing to her family. It honors them. It honors Christ.

This is simply and honestly how it works, friend. If we are not committed to being the redeemed who say so, who earnestly seek to weave the truth of who God is and how He loves into our daily lives, it will be lost on us. It will be lost to our children. An entire generation of faithfulness, the stories of God's enduring goodness could be completely missed because we simply failed to recognize and remember, failed to pay attention and pass it on. Our stories never consist entirely of cookie baking and family campouts. Deena lost a brutal and painful battle with cancer, and yet even in pain, her story was the same. Faithfulness and loving with everything she had.

We must remember the stories of His goodness. We must tell them. We are the redeemed, and it is both our job and our joy to say so.

but then she remembered . . . to say so

G. K. Chesterton makes an interesting point about monotony. (You can find it on page 119.) On a scale of 1 to 10, if 1 is endless repetition and 10 is endless change, where would you prefer to land?

What do you think about Chesterton's idea of monotony in creation and adults not being strong enough to exult in it?

Could the repetitive rhythms of creation be regular reminders for us to pay attention to God? To glory in His sameness?

We are going to kick off this portion of our study with some solid reminders.

First, from Paul.

Read Philippians 3:1 What is Paul's first command?

What are Paul's thoughts on writing the same things?

Next, from Peter.

Read 2 Peter 1:12–15. How is Peter stirring up believers?

What good qualities is he reminding them of? (2 Peter 1:5–8. *Hey, look, it's our memory verse from chapter 4.*)

Why? (vv. 14–15)

Note here how Peter says he is going to *stir them up* and that he will *make every effort* so they can recall truth in the future. **What can you note about Peter's intentionality here?**

And then, from Jude.

Read Jude 5–7. Let's do a little fill-in-the-blank on verse 5 below. (*I'm working with the English Standard Version. The New International Version will be similar. If you are using a different translation, you can either look up one of these translations online or adapt as needed.*)

Now I want to _____ you, although you _____ _____ _____it, that Jesus, who _____ a people out of the land of _____ , afterward _____ those who did not _____.

Remembering just took a serious turn, didn't it? **What is Jude alluding to when he says, "although you once fully knew it"?**

Look over the examples Jude gives in verses 6 and 7. **How would the church have known these stories?**

Go back to verses 3–4. **Why is Jude writing to the church?**

What is threatening the church at this time (v. 4)?

It's interesting that most translations of the Bible use the same word in verse 3. *Contend* for the faith. Vine's Expository Dictionary says it means "to contend about a thing as a combatant—someone engaged in battle."[11] The secular world is pressing down hard on the church, seeping in, and Jude is calling the church to battle, to fight for truth. He begins by reminding them what they seemed to have forgotten.

The Word of God is timeless and timely, friend. Take note.

We are called to be rememberers and relentless sharers of truth. What might this look like practically, in your life?

Matthew Henry said that "under the influence of gospel devotions, we may daily exemplify a gospel conversation."[12] That is a such a beautiful way of putting it. Read Colossians 3:16–17. What is Paul's first instruction in this passage?

He doesn't leave us there. He offers a list of *how* we are to do this. **Write out his list of ideas below.**

Now look at your list. **Take a couple minutes to think how you could actively let the Word of Christ dwell in you richly by doing some of these things. Be specific. Don't worry, you are not signing yourself up for anything; we are just brainstorming what this could look like for now.**

Think back to the last time you studied for something. Maybe it was high school or college or for some professional testing or certification. Were you focused more on encoding or retrieval? (Remember, encoding is essentially getting facts into your brain, while retrieval is getting them out.)

Were you surprised by the impact retrieval has on long-term memory and overall learning?

What impact could that/should that have on how we share our faith?

Attending Deena's funeral was a powerful and poignant reminder for me. Funerals tend to be that way, but this one was different. Maybe I'm just getting older, but there is something beautiful about a life lived quietly and earnestly before the Lord. See 1 Thessalonians 4:11–12. Deena lived this.

The noisy world we live in leads us to believe that we only have value if we are seen, if we have a platform, if we get likes and shares and are known and noticed. It's a lie, friend. Deena had none of that. She lived a beautiful life before the Lord. She was faithful. And that is the story her life will tell for generations. I can only imagine what it was like for her to hear her Savior's *well done*. May we live for the same reward.

In closing here, can we do the sobering work of thinking through how our lives might be remembered? What story do our days tell? What will our friends and families say we loved?

We are the redeemed who have the privilege, honor, and responsibility of saying so. May our days and ways be shaped by and speak of this truth.

7

remembering when you feel weak

Sin is ugly. The older I get, the more I recognize it. The brokenness in our world, in relationships, in creation, it's really horrible. News stories are heavy with world problems and local issues. Some days we can't help but notice the disastrous damage sin continues to have on this world. The discomfort is a visceral reminder—it's not supposed to be this way. It's not.

But much of that ugliness is at arm's length. The more dangerous sin is the one we don't notice, the one that looms quiet and close, comfortable. In his book *Awe*, Paul Tripp calls it spiritual amnesia. "It's the physical ability to see without the spiritual ability to see what you've seen."[1] That's a fantastic description. The physical ability to see is not enough for believers. It's the spiritual ability to see, to know the truth of God's Word and remember it, to let that be the fuel of our faith, to let it imbibe our thoughts and actions, the way we see and hear and respond to the world around us, that changes everything.

In 2 Kings we are told this incredible story of the prophet Elisha. Elisha was a man of God who mentored under the prophet Elijah, which means that he had followed God for some time and had seen His power on display. He had communion with God, knew who He was, and acted in confidence of that truth. In 2 Kings 6 we find the King of Syria trying to stir up trouble with Israel. He would set up camp for a sneak attack on God's people, and every time, the prophet Elisha would somehow, by the Spirit of God, be made aware of these plans. As soon as he did, he would tip off the king of Israel, and Syria's plans would be foiled. Scripture tells us this happened more than once or twice.

You can imagine the Syrian king's frustration. But he really had no clue how it was happening. So he lined up his servants and asked them who the traitor was. He wanted to know who was leaking intel to the enemy. And the servants, they knew exactly who it was. "Elisha, the prophet who is in Israel, tells the king of Israel the words that you speak in your bedroom."[2] Scripture doesn't say, so apparently we don't need to know, but I have to imagine that Syrian king was a bit creeped out right then. Right? I mean, if some random guy is spouting off facts that I share in secret in my bedroom, that would get my attention. But this Syrian king has no clue who he is messing with. So he sends his men to seize Elisha.

Early the next morning, Elisha's servant wakes up to see an army of chariots and horses all around the city. The Syrian king might have been clueless as to the power backing Elisha, but he's not an idiot. He's showing up in force. "Oh, my master, what are we to do?"[3] Elisha's servant pleads. Elisha does what he has always done. He remembers what he knows to be true, and he trains his servant in the process. "He said, 'Do not be afraid, for those who are with us are more than those who are with them.' Then Elisha prayed and said, 'O LORD, please open his eyes that he may see.' So the LORD opened the eyes of the young man and he saw, and behold, the mountain was full of horses and chariots of fire all around Elisha."[4] Isn't that story just incredible, friend? I love it. Elisha didn't ask God to open his own spiritual eyes. He was already there, seeing the world around him that way. He was so chill, so confident in God's provision, so aware of His protection that he took advantage of a powerful teaching moment. He asked God to open his servant's spiritual eyes. He was like *please, God, he's gotta see this.* And He did. Friend, I want to see that. We desperately need spiritual eyes to see the hurt of the world, the fear at our front door, the pain and suffering and bleakness, and the army of God that goes before us there, prevails from the mountain. It changes things. It changes everything. Believers need spiritual eyes to see the world around them rightly and not be dragged down under the weight of it all.

But Home Is Different

I'll be the first to admit I fail at this frequently, but I can tell you God is faithfully sharpening my reflexes. Too many times I have failed to see the holy of the moment in the small tasks of motherhood or life in general. There are dull and dank tasks we all have to do no matter what our "job" is, and they can feel monotonous. Remember, I'm the recovering "Don't waste my time!" mother. I see, but I'm prone to not really seeing because I've got a schedule to keep and things to do.

When the world turns wild, we can feel compelled to watch the news feed obsessively, and we give way to a brooding fear churning deep in us, as if we don't even know where we are going, who we are surrounded by. We have a history! We waste our minutes, fail to value moments, as if we don't know where we are going. We binge watch, impulse shop, and scroll away hours at a time to fill a void because we forget that we are people who know where they are going. Of all people on earth, friend, we know where we are going, and we know exactly Who is with us. We know time matters. We should be people of innate direction. Let the world spin as it may, frazzle and fray, but we need to be the ones who are oriented toward Christ and eternally focused. We cannot afford to be circumstantially oriented. Our knowledge of God and remembrance of Him demand something different.

The most powerful truth I want you to know before we continue, friend, is that God's grace meets us here, and His Holy Spirit empowers us to remembrance. Psalm 103 says that He knows our frame, He remembers that we are dust.[5] I don't think there is a more encouraging Scripture for our sanctification because we mess it all up on the daily. But we have an intimate Creator God who gets our weakness, knows it, and meets us right there. He is the Father God who made a way for all who receive and believe to become children of God. Do you see how He looks on us with both the tenderness and loving guidance of a Father? He calls us higher *and* empowers our obedience as Jesus told us, "But the Helper, the Holy Spirit, whom the Father will send in my name, he will teach you all things and bring to remembrance all that I have said to you."[6] This is good news for us.

We aren't on our own in this huge task of remembering. Your very frame is known, and God has made a way for us to remember Him, remember who we are because of Him, and remember where we are headed.

About Me

Researchers agree that our autobiographical memory, the memory of our personal events and experiences, isn't all that awesome. We might think it is, but we don't always realize all that we have lost, or what details we filter and unknowingly adjust over time. According to the Oxford Handbook of Memory, "An interesting aspect of autobiographic memory is that it is intimately tied to conceptions of self—of who and what we are. Many studies have found memories are reconstructed to satisfy self-serving motives, and that people remember themselves in a more favorable light than is warranted."[7] So once again, the challenge is not only *that* we forget, which we do, but we don't always remember rightly either and have a tendency to puff ourselves up a bit in the process. Pride is a temptation not only in the present, but in how we view our past as well. When we automatically fill our memories with a puffed-up version of ourselves, we fail to remember God was there. We make this messy, don't we?

We probably didn't need the *Oxford Handbook of Memory* to tell us that, though. Who hasn't had a conversation with someone decades past high school who is still weaving those stellar football stats into the conversation? Indeed, we are prone to a little self-serving memory.

A few years ago, Ross and I sat next to a group of grandfather-aged men who were in a lively discussion, rehashing their glory days of outrunning the cops with their muscle cars. I will admit, their stories were entertaining. The world has changed a bit since the *Dukes of Hazzard* days when those gentlemen were young. I asked Ross as we left, "How many of those stories do you think were actually true?" He wisely responded, "I think there was *some* truth in all of them." That autobiographical memory was just doing what it does.

In a 2013 study of individuals with highly superior autobiographical memories, researchers decided they would learn a few things from the best of the best when it comes to memory. These are the people who can remember what they had for lunch on a specific date ten years ago. They are proven rememberers. But even with the breadth of information these superstars could remember, they surprised the researchers when the accuracy of their memories was checked. Overall, the distortion rate in their memories was no different from the average person. Their breadth of recall was impressive, but they missed the details just as frequently as the rest of us.[8] Apparently, this isn't an isolated problem, or a new one.

From the beginning of creation, we haven't been so good at the "seeing spiritually" Tripp references, or the remembering rightly. It's no excuse for us, but it is a fact of our frame. In Deuteronomy 6 God gave Moses wisdom with which to guide his people for this very purpose.

> You shall love the LORD your God with all your heart and with all your soul and with all your might. And these words that I command you today shall be on your heart. You shall teach them diligently to your children, and shall talk of them when you sit in your house, and when you walk by the way, and when you lie down, and when you rise. You shall bind them on as a sign on your hand, and they shall be as frontlets between your eyes. You shall write them on the doorposts of your house and on your gates. . . . Take care lest you forget the LORD, who brought you out of the land of Egypt, out of the house of slavery.[9]

Stay with me, friend, because he's not done. If it feels a little repetitive, I think that just may be part of his point.

> When your son asks you in time to come, "What is the meaning of the testimonies and the statutes and the rules that the LORD our God has commanded you?" then you shall say to your son, "We were Pharaoh's slaves in Egypt. And the LORD brought us out of Egypt with a mighty hand. And the LORD showed signs and wonders, great and grievous, against Egypt and against Pharaoh and all his household, before our eyes. And he brought us out from there, that he might bring us in and give us the land that he swore to give to our fathers. And the LORD commanded us to do all these statutes, to fear the LORD our God, for our good always, that he might preserve us alive, as we are this day. And it will be righteousness for us, if we are careful to do all this commandment before the LORD our God, as he has commanded us."[10]

There are a couple really important things I want us to notice in this passage.

A plan for remembrance has been built into Scripture. The God that knows our frame went before us. He knows our limited nature. He's not surprised by our amnesia. So He laid out instructions for our remembering. You can trace Jesus's words of the first commandment back to the Deuteronomy passage above. According to the count by evangelist George Pentecost, the Old Testament is quoted or alluded to in the New Testament a total of 885 times, giving us not only a picture of the authors' acts of remembrance, but encouraging our own remembering through repetition as well. Even, as we discussed in a previous chapter, at the Last Supper, we see Jesus Christ generously continuing to guide our future remembering, as He said, "Do this in remembrance of me."[11] It should be a comforting assurance to us that God knows our frame and provides for us in order that we may be strengthened by the instruction and remembering of His word.

Memory is an inheritance. The intergenerational exchange should not be overlooked here. Memory is not only for us, but for the future, for our children and our children's children. The solidifying foundation of a generational faith, God's goodness and greatness at work over far more than the tiny timespan of our lives, is a rich gift of both perspective and identity. It's not just a good idea; as believers, it is our responsibility. Do not despair even for a second if this did not occur in your own life, or your own family. It is not a prerequisite, but a gift. Even if a godly heritage is not something you have lived, it is something you can give. Starting now. Let's pass on what is important. Let's be all about it, teaching and talking, rising and walking, passing on truth that must be remembered, daily.

Memory must be the testimony of God's goodness. Remember that autobiographical memory we discussed earlier—the one we are prone to distort? It is our responsibility as believers to remember rightly. Moses's retelling does not run from or gloss over the hard, "We were Pharaoh's slaves in Egypt." We are sometimes tempted to skip or edit the hard from our story because it's not pretty. But neglecting the hard parts of our story would require us to neglect the truth of what God delivered us from. Moses doesn't dwell there, but he certainly doesn't deny it either. We were slaves. Fact. And that is how you are to tell it.

Notice, in summary form, where he goes from here, though: The Lord brought us . . . showed signs . . . that he might bring us . . . give us . . . commanded us . . . that he might preserve us.[12] Tell me, who is this story about? We must remember the story rightly so we can retell it rightly. This is not a story about Moses's excellent leadership qualities or the Israelites's enduring patience or faithfulness. No, that is not how this story went, nor how it is to be retold. This story was to be remembered and retold one way: God did it. That is the story. And it's our story as well. Our testimony will forever be the story of His goodness.

The past has a present and a future. The way this passage ends supersedes time. The discussion is of the past, but its meaning is for that of the present and the future. That is the innate importance of memory—not to bring us back so we can stay there, but to remind us in order that we may move forward rightly. We are called to *zakar*, to remember. "The LORD commanded us to do all these statutes, to fear the LORD our God, for our good always, that he might preserve us alive, as we are this day."[13] This is God relating the past to the present as those mothers and fathers are recounting the past to their children. "And it will be righteousness for us, if we are careful to do all this commandment before the LORD our God, as he has commanded us."[14] Notice the shift to the future tense there: *will be*. It is beautiful and powerful to realize that the God who was the same yesterday, today, and forever instructs us to use the stories of His faithfulness in the past to understand our job in the present so that it may be well with us in the future. He knows our frame. And He sustains.

Unqualified, But Not Disqualified

Look, friend, the realization of our weak frame, our continual acts of forgetfulness or failed remembrance, can be frustrating. I am chief among the frustrated forgetters. Even in menial daily tasks, I am acutely aware of my forgetfulness. Two of my grandmothers passed away with forms of dementia, and that knowledge plays at the edges of my mind, my fears, at times. I'm on the lookout for telltale signs. I recently shared my concerns with some close friends: *"I frequently mess up my kids' names. Words sometimes fail me. Is my mind slipping?"* And they laughed at me in the way only close friends can. "If you're slipping, Katie, we're all slipping." That's a relief. I think.

But it was helpful to share it with them, to trade stories, not only to learn that age seems to be having equal impact on all of us, but that we are handling it quite differently. See, my friends were able to laugh about their occasionally failing minds. They shared funny stories of silly things they said or random things they forgot, and they laughed some more. I, however, had been quite frustrated by similar experiences. Because I was a little bit worried, I was irritated each time something slipped my mind. I never laughed in a moment of forgetfulness. I almost unknowingly let it settle into fear, into evidence that the worst-case scenario is true. I'm a hopeless forgetter.

The bad news is, it's true. The signs I might barely be showing on the physical level are fully true at a spiritual level. I'm a hopeless forgetter who is prone to question God's goodness when a school gets shot up, doubt His direction when the desert seems long, wonder about His provision when our finances feel tight. I have both a history and heritage of nothing less than His unfailing love, and yet the distraction of my present circumstances consumes my gaze. Fast forgetfulness becomes a failure to pay attention, to remember who God was and is and will be in whatever this situation may be. We forget who God is and how He loves. We scale Him small, sell Him short, and live completely ignorant of how big He really is. We're blind to the blessings, to the protection and provision He affords us through means we fail to understand. *He is good.* And we are so often tempted to believe otherwise.

That's the bad news, friend. But the good news is, He meets us even here. Just as He met a young servant, scared stiff staring at the enemy surrounding the city in 2 Kings, He meets us right here in our weakness. He doesn't despise our fragile frame; He knows it, as the Psalmist says. He gets it and moves toward us in both mercy and power. That is good news.

Coming Up Short

It's hard be the youngest. I see it on occasion in my nine-year-old son, the baby. Sure, there are all kinds of advantages to being the little guy with three older siblings to look up to, but sometimes it's just hard. Today was one of those days. Bo got a journal recently and has been all about recording the highlights of his days. He writes about having friends over, about what we had for dinner, and his baseball games—*"I got to play catcher and made the final out!!!"* All the nine-year-old exclamation points, of course.

But after about a week of journaling, Bo announced he didn't want to do it anymore. Nine-year-olds can be prone to dropping hobbies after a solid week of commitment, so I didn't think much about it until I noticed the look on his face. Emotion was brimming in his eyes, a little tremble played at his lips. "What's wrong, buddy? What happened with the journaling?" I pried. "I'm terrible at it!" he declared. "My writing is messy, and I just keep making a mess of it all." He quickly went in search of evidence and returned with pages of the cutest little boy handwriting (said the mom). He had marked out misspelled words when he caught them, drew the occasional picture when he thought to, and he offered it all to me as confirmation that he was indeed terrible at journaling.

It was sad to watch. This boy who was so excited about journaling just a week ago, eager to capture his days and make a little record for himself, was now fully convinced that he was a failure at journaling. He told me that he doesn't write neatly, that all of his older siblings write better than he does, and that he messes up all the time and makes his pages messy. His sisters don't do that, he noted. He's just "no good at it."

Here's the thing: There were threads of truth in his observations. He was correct, his older siblings don't write like a nine-year-old. And his pages were somewhat messy. Correcting our mistakes can come out that way. I couldn't argue with that. But the biggest truths Bo was missing was the fact that He *is* nine. He *is* a beginner. He *is* still learning how to do this well. He wasn't paying attention when his older siblings were learning how to write; he was busy playing with blocks. And now he was comparing his beginning with someone else's middle. He lost patience with his own learning. He wasn't being fair to himself, to his growing, to his frame. I could meet him with all the compassion and honesty in the world, but if he stays bent on disqualifying himself, there is not much I could do about it.

I have to wonder how many times we're all like Bo. Our journals are probably tidier, with a few less scribbles and drawings, but how often do we get frustrated with our mistakes, with our real growing and learning as we follow Christ, so in shame we disqualify ourselves from relationship with Him? How often do we compare ourselves to Christians who have spent years faithfully growing in maturity, and become embarrassed by our own humble beginning with the Lord? How often, in our fight against sin, do we feel like one giant disappointment to God? Too often. Whatever your answer, it's too often.

Look, we are told in Proverbs to fear the Lord and hate what is evil.[15] James instructed that we submit ourselves to God and resist the devil.[16] In Genesis, we are reminded that sin is crouching at our door, it desires to have us, but we must rule over it.[17] God doesn't make light of sin, and therefore we shouldn't either. Remember, Bo's journal was indeed messy. We can't negate facts. But it is equally foolish to create a false dichotomy. God sees our sins and knows our weaknesses, and still, when we are repentant, getting real about our mistakes and real about our need for Him, He moves in a mighty rush of mercy toward us. He knows our frame, and He loves us still. This is good news, friend.

John reminds the body of believers (and us) that if we confess our sins, He is faithful and just to forgive our sins and cleanse us from all unrighteousness. This is the process. This is what He does and how He loves. *Do you believe it?* We must not refuse His mercy toward us by our unbelief. He knows your frame, friend. He made you. And just as soon as you ask, He has forgiven you. Wholly, fully, completely. What would it look like to live from that truth?

The Invitation of Weakness

I want to give you a picture of what we are discussing here in the life of Christ. This is one you likely know, but . . . wait for it . . . may have failed to remember. Beginning just before the Passover feast—the last meal Jesus would celebrate with His disciples—John opens chapter 13 of his gospel with a beautiful statement I don't want us to miss. "Jesus knew that his hour had come to leave this world and return to his Father. He loved his disciples during his ministry on earth, and now he loved them to the very end."[18] Isn't that beautiful? The full weight, the full ache, of the sacrifice that Jesus will soon make is beginning to settle in. He felt it. But still, He loved. To the very end, He loved.

And even there, His love was action. In that moment, Jesus rose and poured water into a basin. He knelt before every single one of His disciples and began washing their feet. All twelve of them. The ache of imminent betrayal, the burden for what sin would cost, did not overcome Christ; love did. Even before Judas, Jesus knelt, and He loved. Matthew Henry says of the disciples, "They were weak and defective in knowledge and grace, dull and forgetful; and yet, though he reproved them often, he never ceased to love them and take care of them."[19] Nothing of their own merit made them lovable; Christ did.

That is hard to comprehend, isn't it? His love is greater than we even know. He knew His disciples. He knows us. And to the end, He loves.

A little later that evening Jesus begins to let His disciples know what is ahead. "Truly, truly, I say to you, one of you will betray me."[20] And they all look around trying to figure out who it might be. In his gospel, Matthew says they were very sorrowful and began to say to Him, "Is it I, Lord?"[21] What a humble question. Not one of the disciples was perfect. They loved Jesus, but they also were aware of their own temptation to sin. They knew their frame. They didn't believe it was them, but while the question hung in the air, they definitely wanted to make certain it was not.

Friend, this exchange is important for many reasons. But what I want you to note right now is how Jesus Christ responds to His imperfect followers. I want you to see how He moves toward them. I want you to see His offering extended to them, all of them, even as He knows one of them is about to choose to reject Him. He knew their frame. And to the very end, He met them there, showing love and offering mercy. He does the very same for you and me.

In his second letter to the church at Corinth, Paul talks about some sort of ailment he has—"a thorn in my flesh," Paul calls it. He pleads to God for reprieve, several times, and Paul records God's response to him as "My grace is sufficient for you, for my power is made perfect in weakness."[22] So Paul makes up his mind to view it differently. "Therefore I will boast all the more gladly of my weaknesses, so that the power of Christ may rest upon me. For the sake of Christ, then, I am content with weaknesses, insults, hardships, persecutions, and calamities. For when I am weak, then I am strong."[23] Paul figured it out, friend. Let's learn it right along with him.

Stop counting losses. Stop tracking them with tally marks and measuring all the places you don't quite add up. That's losing math for all of us. There are times we cannot sit ten minutes with the Bible open in our laps and remember that we were here to pray, that we want to seek the Lord. Our brains wander so quickly in another direction, *again*. It feels like failure. And perhaps it is, but we must refuse to make failure final, because Christ does not. He meets the weak-framed and speaks life to them, loves them. *Loves us.*

Christ addressed Thomas's doubts with directness, but also a gentle nearness, in peace.[24] He met the Samaritan woman, caught up in her well-known sin, with a dignity that she would not have been afforded elsewhere. And with compassion, He called her higher. This is the Christ who offers to us all, "Come to me, all who are weary and heavy-laden, and I will give you rest."[25] He himself endured temptation, and He is able to help those who are being tempted. Friend, we have a Savior who knows our frame because He chose to live within the confines of it as well. What a Savior, what a friend.

We have a choice in our remembering. We can see the limits and confines of our design and be continually frustrated. We can know the horrors of our past, the mountain of bad decisions and failed attempts, and refuse to remember. We can refine and edit the past, perhaps put a filter on it to tidy it up a little, or we can insert ourselves a little more to boast in our own heroics. Or, by the grace of God and the power of the Holy Spirit, we can remember rightly. We can look to the One who understands the frailty of our frame and reminds us that His power is made perfect right there. We can tell and retell the story of what He has done throughout history and generations so that His goodness in the past will be known in the present and carried into every tomorrow. We serve a mighty and faithful God, friend. That is a story worth sharing.

but then she remembered . . . He knows her frame

Let's talk about that story of Elisha in 2 Kings 6. Isn't it incredible? For a look at the prophet's roots, go back and read 2 Kings 2:1–14. **Who was Elisha's mentor?**

What was Elisha's last request of his mentor (2 Kings 2:9)?

What is the powerful ending to this portion of Scripture in verse 14?

Read the next verse. **What do the sons of the prophets, who have been observing this whole interaction at a distance (v. 7), say of Elisha in verse 15?**

We learned about seeing with spiritual eyes through the story of Elisha in 2 Kings 6. Elisha prayed that his servant would be able to see the angel armies, and God opened his eyes so he could see a mountain full of horses and chariots of fire surrounding them. But we left the story there—with the Syrian army surrounding and the army of God on the mountain. Let's trek back there. Read 2 Kings 6:8–23 to get a sense of the story. How did this confrontation with the Syrian army end?

Elisha was a man who had clearly done time with God. He knows Him, remembers what He has done, asks for more of His Spirit, and acts in confidence because he knows Who is with him.

Let's take a look at Deuteronomy 6 and see how it relates to remembering. This is hope for all of us who feel terrible at remembering. God knows, and He gives us instruction on how we can do this well. Read Deuteronomy 6:4–9.

What are God's people commanded to do (v. 5)?

Where are the commands supposed to be stored (v. 6)?

The word used for "heart" above is quite common in Scripture. Its Hebrew root is *lebab*, which can also refer to the mind and soul, the center for understanding. In English when we say something is "on our heart," we tend to refer to the emotional side of things, but Moses is commanding that these words be placed in the heart and mind and soul, that they be understood and remembered. Like when my daughter says she knows her piano piece by heart—that is the heart we are talking about here. So how are they to do this? Read verses 7–9 and make note of the verbs and the timing below, the how and when of this passage.

Keep right on going and read the caution in verses 10–13. **Which cities does Moses speak of (v. 10)?**

Which houses is he talking about (v. 11)?

Which vineyards and olive trees is he making note of (v. 11)?

God is making a clear point by way of Moses. He has provided in miraculous ways for His people. They are about to reap an enormous blessing on no account of their own good work. He knows their frame, and He wants them to remember rightly.

We can't stop there, because Moses doesn't stop there. Moses wants to drive this point home. Jump to verses 20–25 in chapter 6 and read. Moses is instructing the people on dialogue with their children, on remembering and stating the facts rightly. In verse 21 he begins with "We were Pharaoh's slaves in Egypt . . ." **Hunt for every subject and verb after that and list them below.**

How is Moses teaching the Israelites about the retelling? Who is this story about?

What can we learn here? What story are we passing on?

The details may be different, but much is the same—deliverance, provision, protection. Who is the author of your story? Are you remembering and retelling it rightly?

Disqualified. Have you ever been disqualified from something? When I first began writing, I asked to join a Christian bloggers group online. I don't recall the details of the group, but it was some sort of cohort of beginning writers who supported and learned from one another. A writing friend had encouraged me to join. In order to gain access to this community, connected via a private Facebook group, prospects had to answer a host of questions and submit their website for review. Apparently, they had a vetting process to ensure the community was like-minded. I followed the rules, answered the questions, and a couple days later I received a gracious denial. *Thank you for your interest in our group, but your website and content is not overtly Christian enough.* Huh. Friend, my faith has always been the heart of my writing. I've never written about anything else. So this one stung for a minute. Of all the things a person could fail at, could be disqualified by—*I wasn't Christian enough.* What does that even mean?

Too often though we don't need someone else to disqualify us, like Bo with his journal. Instead, we grab a gavel and make the declaration ourselves. Take a minute to read through Romans 8:31–39 and fill in the blanks in the specific verses below:

Verses 31–32

If _____ is for us, who can be _____ us? He who did not spare his own _____ but gave him up for _____ _____, how will he not also with him graciously give us _____ _____?

Verse 35

Who shall _____ us from the love of Christ? Shall _____, or _____, or _____, or _____, or _____, or _____, or _____?

Verse 37–39

_____, in all these things we are more than _____ through him who _____ _____. For I am _____ that neither _____ nor _____, nor _____ nor _____, nor things _____, nor

things _____ _____, nor _____, nor _____ nor _____,
nor anything else in all creation, will be able to _____ us from
the _____ of God in Christ Jesus our Lord.

Romans 8 is a powerful reminder, friend. No one can disqualify you
when Christ has called you His own.

One last task, and you don't even need a pen for this one. I want you
to find John 13 in your Bible and read verses 1–20. Read through how
Jesus loved His own in the world and loved them to the very end. Imagine
yourself in that gathering. Jesus stooping low, drawing near, to love you
too. He knows your frame, and He meets you there. Remember that.

Take a minute to thank God for how He knows and how He loves.
Ask Him, by the power of His Holy Spirit, to seed this truth deep in your
heart, to dispel lies that you might be hanging on to—that you might
know His truth by heart, and remember.

8

habit forming

training to become rememberers

I never think about making my bed each morning. Or starting the dishwasher in the evening. Or how to drive my car, unless the roads are slick and unfamiliar. I don't think much about how to make French toast, how to wrap a gift, or even which keys to type on the keyboard when I'm writing. When was the last time you thought about how to tie your shoes? Our brains are effective at creating neural pathways, the skids of which are greased with usage to the point that they operate with very little resistance, on autopilot almost. They move with efficiency, mostly unimpeded, undemanding.

The process behind this efficiency is commonly called habit, and it is God's masterful design. Our brains, and thus our bodies, can learn to move with efficiency, demanding far less energy as acquired skill becomes memorized. I watched my son learn to drive not too long ago. I saw his neck and shoulders stiffen as he tried to make himself comfortable in the driver's seat, his fingers lock tight around the steering wheel. The remembered feeling came rushing back to me. When I was Tyler's age, my own dad kept gently coaxing me from the passenger's seat of my family's Buick. "Relax," he would tell me. It seemed like an impossible suggestion. How was I supposed to relax? Newly crowned with a training permit, I drove the freeway to the big city, forty-five minutes or so, and as soon as we arrived, I wanted to take a nap from the exhaustion of it all. Paying attention, learning, is exhausting.

But our brains and bodies do learn new rhythms in time. The newness wears off, the necessary movements become learned and remembered, and soon enough it all begins to function quite well in the background. When the neural connections become well established, byways require far less effort. I no longer need a nap to drive the distance. That is certainly helpful. I can drive home without thinking much about the skills required to do so. Helpful. Sometimes I pull into my driveway and wonder how exactly I got home; I was never once thinking about driving. Only a tad bit concerning.

This is precisely how habits work once they are formed. The path of least resistance becomes organic automation for better or for worse. You may not even realize that you bite your nails when you are anxious, that you pick up your phone when you are lonely or avoiding mentally demanding work, or that you shop or clean or become impatient when you are nervous. These are well-greased-skid sorts of habits that feel almost involuntary over time. In his book *Habits of Grace*, David Mathis says, "More than 99 percent of our daily decisions about this and that happen without any immediate reflection. We just act. Our lives flow from the kind of person we are—the kind of person we have become—rather than some succession of time-outs for reflection."[1] That is interesting to think about it, isn't it? It is *necessarily* true. We don't have time to immediately reflect on every single daily decision. If so, we'd navigate all of life like a brand-new driver—stiff necked, white-knuckled, and ready for a nap after forty-five minutes.

However, knowing this beautiful automation that allows so much multiplicity and complexity in our daily lives makes the "kind of person we are—the kind of person we have become," even more important. Do you see that? We live much of our lives and make most of our decisions predicated on the autopilot of this person we have become. When I'm driving and not actively thinking about it, I'm relying on the type of driver I have become. When I'm parenting a teen through a relational issue while making dinner for my family and greeting my husband as he walks through the door, all while the nine-year-old plays his drums in the background, the way I am engaging with each of these people is relying very heavily on the kind of person I have become. Realizing this makes Scriptures, such as Paul's instruction to "walk in a manner worthy of the calling to which have you been called,"[2] come alive. He is giving instruction for our becoming.

Becoming

In Romans chapter 11, Paul is talking to the Gentile believers in Rome about their place in the family of Christ, about what it means to be grafted in by a holy God. As chapter 12 opens, Paul does not mince words as he calls these very believers (and us) higher: "I appeal to you therefore, brothers, by the mercies of God, to present your bodies as a living sacrifice, holy and acceptable to God, which is your spiritual worship. Do not be conformed by the pattern of this world, but be transformed by the renewal of your mind, that by testing you may discern what is the will of God, what is good and acceptable and perfect."[3]

Matthew Henry parses this passage out a bit, saying, "The mind is the acting, ruling part of us; so that the renewing of the mind is the renewing of the whole man, for out of it are the issues of life."[4] This transformation Paul speaks of occurs in a mind that *refuses* to be shaped by the world, but rather one that is renewed, sanctified, by the truth. *This* mind is empowered to test and discern the will of God. Our understanding of the very good, acceptable, and perfect will of God is dependent upon and clarified by what we are being shaped by. The well-worn paths we are choosing to slide down are more important than we realize. They are shaping us, forming us, training us. In a world determined to shape us, it is vital that we commit to being shaped by the Word.

The trouble is that we are a bit resistant to the idea of training. We can hear *another* sermon, read *another* article on the importance of Bible reading, and it somehow converts to the exact sound of the voice of Charlie Brown's teacher. If you know, you know. We can hear about the importance of prayer and talking to God, and it sounds like the LMNOP of the Christian alphabet: It's so common, it all runs together. Christian-read-Bible-pray. Yes, *we know*. And when we hear someone drone on about memorization, well, break out the felt board, friend, because most of us haven't done that since Sunday school. And it's hard. And we're old(er). And it's hard(er).

We not only think this sort of training is outdated or we don't have the time for such training, we not only tend to tune this idea out because it feels a bit overplayed, but it can feel formulaic, a bit like legalism. We are the freedom-in-Christ culture. It is for freedom that we are set free, and we don't need another Bible-reading checklist. No. Thank you, but no. *But wait.* We are tempted to warp Scripture to our own demise here. Our freedom is from the ceremonial law to Christ, our great high priest. Hebrews says we have a high priest who is able to sympathize with our weaknesses (remember, He knows our frame) and because of that, because of the gospel, we have freedom of access. We get freedom to know Him, to draw near to the throne of grace and find mercy and grace in our time of need. Life is tough, friend. Why *wouldn't* we make drawing near our habit?

I once heard Costi Hinn give a stellar analogy that I have found helpful. Think for a minute about a quarterback on a football team. He runs the offense and leads his team. He has a job to do, and he is expected to show up and get it done every week. But that is not all that is expected of him—far from it. He calls the plays in the huddle and is expected to show up prepared to do so. It is expected that he will know the routes so that he can find the open teammate as quickly as possible. It is expected that he will know his options within each play and be trained to recognize alternatives when necessary. We expect nothing less from a quarterback. Train, show up, be prepared, be ready.

But what if the quarterback wasn't? What if he didn't train and practice? What if he refused to watch film and learn the plays? What if he showed up completely unprepared? He likely wouldn't have a job, right? He wouldn't thrive. His play would be disastrous, and he would let his teammates, who count on and depend on and benefit from his skills, down. Preparation is an understood part of the job. A quarterback's continual training is inherent to his optimal performance. Now, this analogy only goes so far, because our salvation is a gift of Christ's work, not our own, but our response matters. And, as believers, we have been given the gift of the Holy Spirit who empowers us to live out this high calling to glorify our Creator with faithfulness. So why, when it comes to our necessary training and preparation as believers, do we ignore it or call it legalism?

A Different Take

What if it never was about a checklist? What if being faithful was never supposed to be about perfect church attendance, being a stellar no-skip Bible reader, or a memorization master? What if this is really about getting to know your Savior, learning to love Him faithfully, developing patterns of habit that use the very best of our created design to lead us relentlessly, persistently, and consistently to Him? What if becoming disciplined in pursuing Christ was not really about the present, about how I feel right now or what I need right now, but about remembering the God of the past who says He is faithful and just to forgive us when we come to Him in confession—the God who says He hears and heals when His people pray and seek and turn?[5] Can we show up in faithfulness and trust that sowing seeds of relationship and intimacy looks like time spent now and fruit grown both now and later? The God of the past, who is forever unchanging, meets us in the present and changes our future forever. We get to know Him. And it is to our highest advantage and His glory that we get serious about it.

Paul liked athletic analogies as well. He prodded the church in Corinth by reminding them that "Every athlete exercises self-control in all things. They do it to receive a perishable wreath, but we an imperishable. So I do not run aimlessly; I do not box as one beating the air. But I discipline my body and keep it under control, lest after preaching to others I myself should be disqualified."[6] The New Living Translation of this passage says, "I discipline my body like an athlete, training it to do what it should." That plain talk is helpful, isn't it? Paul knows that we are made to glorify God. Sin has broken that process. Temptation is real. So Paul is telling us he works at it, he exercises authority over his body. He is training to show up prepared.

Paul is acutely aware of our proneness to wander mentally, and he's doing something about it. Our days are numbered, and we don't serve anyone well when we spend them beating the air. We are called to set our eyes not on that which is seen and transient, but on that which the Word says is imperishable and eternal.[7] This isn't always instinctive, but it can become our habit. Our remembering of the past serves a present purpose. We are training for the future. We must train ourselves to run with purpose, friend.

Becoming disciplined in growing in Christ's likeness does not have to become dogmatic list-checking. The heart behind dogmatic checklists is not truly bent on honoring Christ anyhow. It's bent on checking that list. What if your husband showed up tonight with a gorgeous bouquet of flowers and said, "I got you these flowers because it's on my checklist of things to do." And he abruptly went about his business for the evening? There is no relationship that thrives in detached list checking. God is not mocked.[8]

But at the same time, healthy habits formed in a heart that truly seeks relationship with Christ is of great gain. Just as bedtime routines prepare our bodies for rest, routines of meeting with the Lord faithfully prepare our hearts to meet and know Him daily, to learn and hear from Him via His word by the power of the Holy Spirit. Being faithful in our Bible reading trains our minds in truth and makes way for us to learn and grow in the grace and knowledge of our Lord and Savior as we have been instructed to do. And committing God's Word to memory gives us a deeper well of truth to draw from even when our Bibles are not available to us.

On Short Notice

This morning some dear friends of mine, Ryan and Alesha, are on a plane headed across the Pacific Ocean to South Korea. After a mandated quarantine, they will begin legal proceedings to give two-year-old Hana a new last name; she will become theirs. *Finally.* Adoption is no small process. International adoption is even less small. International adoption in the time of COVID? I've never walked that road, but I can tell you as a front-row praying friend, it has often felt like a standstill, like rush hour deadlock with only minor surges and still more delays. Up until last week, that is, when Alesha received a brief email. *"We need you here for court, in 8 days."* Eight days to get tickets and fly across the world. Eight days to arrange childcare for the kids that will stay at home, to get substitutes at work and rearrange schedules and plan meals and prepare and pack. Eight days until they would step foot in their soon-to-be daughter's homeland for the very first time, prepare to meet her, introduce themselves as her stranger-parents, and proceed with faith that the God who adopted them would by the power of His Holy Spirit enable them to love this little one as their own too. They said, "Of course!"

Yesterday afternoon Alesha and I made time for a walk before her big trip. I've been walking with her for almost two decades now. We've walked through pregnancies, births, and losses. We've walked through toddlers and teenagers. But this international adoption, *"I'm headed to Korea tomorrow to gain a daughter,"* this was new. So I asked her how she has been processing the past week of her life and all that is ahead. She told me she felt panicky at first. Eight days felt far too sudden, and everything seemed immediately urgent. But after a day or two, the intensity of her emotions started to settle. She began to recall and remember how far God had brought them. She started to sleep better at night and wake feeling rested again, and each day after that she began to witness God bringing every single detail into place. "This week has been incredible," she told me.

There have been moments when the panic seeks to return, she admitted. When the challenges seem too great or the tired gets real, and there is a nagging temptation to be overwhelmed. But she has gotten better at quieting her heart and forcing herself to remember who God is. She chooses to remember how God has loved them and been faithful to them through every step of this process. And from there she can choose to trade panic for praise because she knows who God will be in and through every tomorrow. My friend Alesha, she is in training. She *has been* training for the past twenty years that I have known her. She disciplines her mind and body. She refuses to beat the air. Every time the temptation for fear and worry surfaces, she chooses to remember who God is. And by the grace of God, she is doing it incredibly well.

You and I don't have to go through an international adoption to learn this. Hopelessness can leach into a marriage and doubt can take hold. Loneliness can disease any relationship and we can feel that God has forsaken us. Financial challenges can weigh heavy, political tensions can breed confusion, and physical illness can send suffocating fear coursing through our very veins. The challenges vary, but each one comes with the temptation to worry and fret, to mill and stew, to run aimlessly, in Paul's words, as our heart and mind seek to fixate on the challenge in front of us instead of the God who goes before us. Before the panic hits, and when it does, we have a choice.

Captive

Jeremiah models this choice for us in the book of Lamentations. The whole book is inked under the desperate weight of captivity. Israel has forsaken the Lord and intense suffering results. We studied Deuteronomy 6 in chapter 7 and learned how God laid out a beautifully specific plan for His people's remembering, but in Jeremiah 2 we see what choice they ultimately made:

> "They did not say, 'Where is the LORD who brought us up from the land of Egypt, who led us in the wilderness, in a land of deserts and pits, in a land of drought and deep darkness, in a land that none passes through, where no man dwells?' And I brought you into a plentiful land to enjoy its fruits and its good things. But when you came in, you defiled my land and made my heritage an abomination."[9]

The disappointment in this passage is palpable. God had a plan for their future. He provided a plan for their remembrance and their children's and their children's children. But now their heritage has become an abomination—detestable, some translations say. A disgusting thing.

In the book of Lamentations, Jeremiah is lamenting the destruction of Jerusalem during the Babylonian invasion. But the hinge of the book comes midway through in chapter 3. Jeremiah says, "Remember my affliction and my wanderings, the wormwood and the gall! My soul continually remembers it and is bowed down within me."[10] The prophet is leveling with us here. The suffering is unforgettable. He acknowledges it. He feels the full weight of it, but he doesn't stop there. "But this I call to mind, and therefore I have hope: The steadfast love of the LORD never ceases; his mercies never come to an end; they are new every morning; great is your faithfulness. 'The LORD is my portion,' says my soul, 'therefore I will hope in him.'"[11] Jeremiah knows he has a choice in the matter. He has trained his mind to recall who God is, how he loves, and therefore, even in real and devastating loss, he has hope for today and tomorrow, and he continues on in the following verses praising the goodness of God.

I hope you are beginning to see how this works, friend. We have a choice—a choice that can become a chosen reflex, a habit wrought through faithful practice, training. We have good work to do in season and out, and we have been told to be ready. That means now, today, we are to work on our readiness. We can't just save it for Sunday mornings. Both the mission and the interference are just too great. John Mark Comer candidly states that "Often we come to church hoping for a God hit—a fleeting moment of connection to God before we return to the secular wasteland . . . the problem is more our absence than His, more about our distraction than his disconnection."[12] That's a word, friend. And too often true. A fleeting hit of God is not nearly enough to sustain us through devastating circumstances. And it is nothing less than disobedience when we know the first commandment is to love the Lord our God with everything. We are made to know Him. Let's aim higher. Let's start trying for everything.

Discipline, for Beginners

There is no lack of books and blogs and instruction in the spiritual disciplines. They have found a resurgence in popularity in recent years, so I won't attempt to emulate them. Seek them out if you want to dig deeper. Just be careful of your sources. Be wise and discerning. Not all are equal. For the purposes of this book, however, I want to help you in the basics. I want to help you get started. Think of this as your Couch to 5K in pursuing Christ by forming strong spiritual habits. This is an abridged survey. These tips are suited for the beginner, but I promise they will provide a good workout for those of you who have already established a habit as well.

Many years ago, shortly after I got married, I met a few older women in my church who I was so impressed by. Wisdom seemed to just roll off their tongues as they spoke about the world, about their work, about their marriages or families. They prayed with a humble fervor of belief, and Scripture imbued their words, informed their opinions. I was in awe of them. I remember asking a friend of mine, *How do we get there? How will we ever possibly know that much?* And it was at that time that my friend and I chose to become as faithful as we could about pursuing and knowing Christ. We became committed to learning, to growing slow fruit, to studying and practicing the disciplines listed below. And almost twenty years later, I can tell you, it's adding up. We haven't *arrived*; our journey in knowing Christ is endless, but Scripture is now imbuing *our* thoughts and informing *our* opinions in ever increasing ways. Memorized verses are stacking up and we are seeing in our homes and in our families how His Word does not return void. Disciplining our hearts and minds to be faithfully active about pursuing Christ is a lifelong and bountiful investment. Let's get started.

Read the Word—really

The goal is to make a habit of reading God's Word. We know as believers we are instructed to do so. We know this is a means to knowing God. We know it's the sword of the Spirit. We know and we know and yet . . . we don't *do*. Research shows that 82 percent of Christian Americans read their Bibles only on Sundays while in church.[13] Clearly, we haven't formed the habit. Let's change that. It really isn't all that difficult; we just need to get up the gumption and start. So here's what I want you to do: **Make up your mind.** Start there. No one can choose this for you, but we are pretty good at getting done what we really want to get done. Next, **pick a time.** Choose a time you can be consistent and faithful with. Life happens and schedules get complicated, but we all have spaces that are mostly consistent. Pick that one.

Next, **pick a cue.** Habit loops always involve a cue—something that triggers your mind to engage. I make my bed every single day after I get out of the shower. Stepping out of my bathroom is my cue. I can't help but see the unmade bed in front of me, and I choose to make it. Each morning I pour a cup of coffee and move to my spot on the couch. My Bible waits for me on the coffee table, often open. I sit quietly for a moment and then I read, every day much the same. Cues become the well-greased skids of habit formation. They don't need to be complicated, only consistent. What are you going to attach your Bible reading to? What will you do after or before? You need a solid cue. Next, **develop a routine.** This is the real habit-forming part, when the synapses in our brain connect over time and make the whole process more efficient. Grab the same Bible, or sit in the same chair, or retreat to the same room. It doesn't have to be an involved process, it just has to be the same. Sameness establishes the routine. Routine is what we are after. If you've spent time with children, you know they thrive on morning and bedtime routines (sometimes elaborate ones that drive their parents a little bonkers), but adults aren't all that different. Habits are formed in the flow of consistent routine. Make this happen the same time each day as much as possible, and the flow of your day, the morning or afternoon or evening light, the hunger that comes near lunchtime, will become innate cues pointing you toward your routine. Done consistently, your routine will quickly cease to be a forced path and instead become a welcomed anchor in your day, your new normal.

Finally, **pick a reward**. This is more of a technical term than a traditional understanding of the word *reward*, but logistically it functions as a trigger for your brain to know this pattern is worth remembering. Years ago my friend Susan was teaching me the importance of reading the psalms. She reads a psalm every single day, no matter what else she is studying. She simply reads one psalm until she has read them all, and then she starts over again. But here is the pertinent part for what we are learning here: Each time she reads a psalm, she places a tally mark by the psalm number. Susan formed this habit years ago, and when she opened her Bible to the book of Psalms, I saw dozens of hand-marked tallies by every single chapter. What a powerful reminder of the places you have been with God in His word! Pick a very simple reward. Our brains like them.

That's it. You are all set. Now, you just need to pick a really doable portion of Scripture to begin with and get started. This method is completely flexible. You can read a verse, a chapter, or an entire book at a time. Start small. The goal is a tiny, successful habit, but know this method will grow when you are ready. Just form the habit. I have provided some more resources at the end of this chapter to help you get started.

Pray

Confession time: How many times have you told someone you would pray for them but never did? How many times have you hit that little praying hands emoji or typed the words "Praying for you!" and knew as you were doing it, that it was more of a cordiality than any real course of committed action for you? As believers, prayer is not optional. It is our conversation with God. And it is necessary for right relationship with Him. Oswald Chambers wisely said, "We generally look upon prayer as a means of getting things for ourselves, whereas the biblical idea of prayer is that God's holiness, purpose, and wise order may be brought about."[14] David Mathis says, "Prayer is not finally about getting things from God, but getting God."[15] Getting God. Do we understand what a privilege this is? Getting God is the heart of prayer.

We are told in 1 Thessalonians 5 to pray without ceasing. Continual conversation with God is our goal. But it is also helpful for believers to make intentional times of prayer, to make our requests known to God, and you know, pray for those people we actually said we would. Form your prayer habit in the same manner you did your new Bible reading habit above, only make your Bible reading habit your cue. Simply pray after you finish reading. And keep it very simple. I promise God is not up there with a stopwatch. He rewards those who earnestly seek Him. He loves to respond when His children draw near. Start small, just start. We'll talk more about this in the study section.

Memorize

While this is not a traditional spiritual discipline, it's a very important one that much of the church has relegated to childhood. Even so, neuroscience has shown that memorization increases the plasticity of our brain, meaning, essentially, that the brain in turn responds better.[16] It becomes more adaptable to training, like exercise, almost. Of course, God would create our brains to respond to the commands of His word. Memorization is how we can hide God's word in our hearts; it is one way we invite His words to abide in us. In memorizing Scripture, we are innately meditating on it, committing truth to our minds over and over until it sticks. His words increasingly become our words as Scripture comes out in our prayers and in our conversation with others. Memorizing Scripture is a deep well of provision we neglect.

Darlene Deibler Rose, an American missionary who spent four years in a Japanese prison camp during WWII, writes in her biography, "Paul, the apostle, wrote that it was through the comfort of the Scriptures that he had hope and steadfastness of heart to believe God. I had never needed the Scriptures more than in these months on death row, but since so much of His Word was there in my heart, it was not the punishment the Kemeitai had anticipated when they took my Bible."[17] Darlene Deibler Rose remained nourished, remained hopeful and steadfast because of the Word she had hidden in her heart. We never know what circumstances in our lives might require us to tap in to that store, friend, but I want to be ready when the time comes.

Adore

Adoration is the way we take our quiet time into the full reach of our day. It is intentionally drilling down to smaller bites to, as my friend Sara says, wrestle with a part of God's Word or character. It's saying the truth of who He is and how He loves back to our own hearts and back to Him. Adoration becomes our conversation.

We can adore Him in word or in song. It can come by our pens or through our lips, but it always comes from a heart that desires to engage Christ, to ascribe glory to Him just as we see the psalmists do in Scripture. When we become intentional in this habit, we choose our focus for the day, rather than letting the day choose for us. We plant our feet and invite the Holy Spirit to teach us where He leads us, in the carpool and while we are loading the Whirlpool, as we run errands and run the business. In adoration, we stake a claim to know Christ more, in minutes and margins that we reclaim for relationship with Him, rather than giving away to ever-present distraction at hand.

Fast

Fasting is a physical means of going without in order to more completely focus on Christ. It is forcing a holy discontent in order to know Him and hear Him more clearly, to devote ourselves to Him more fully. We see it practiced in both the Old and New Testaments, and in the Sermon on the Mount we hear Jesus speak of it not as an option, but as an expectation in the life of believers—not an *if* but a *when*.

Fasting is another powerful and underutilized tool in the life of the believer. It can be practiced regularly, as it is now quite common for both protestants and Catholics to do during Lent, but we also see it utilized in Scripture in times of greater need. We see Nehemiah do this when he received the news of the desolate state of Jerusalem. His heart was heavy, and he sought God with fervor through prayer and fasting. Fasting is less habit and more training, although we will fight already established habits in order to go without, but we have the help of the Holy Spirit in doing so, and that interaction is part of the fruit of this training.

One caution to consider. Fasting is a discipline that has become trendy in recent years, although more for health reasons than for spiritual ones. I have read the secular research and understand the digestive, mental, and overall health benefits of periodically limiting food intake. It makes sense that what God calls us to do is also physically and mentally for our good. But fasting for spiritual reasons comes from a different heart position, and I wonder if fasting's current popularity has caused us to blur the intentions, the heart behind the discipline. We would be wise to be honest with ourselves, to ask, "What is my real intent behind this?" Matthew Henry says that "fasting puts an edge on our devout affections."[18] If you have ever fasted, you will likely agree; you have felt that edge. It is vital, in the life of the believer, to expose what those devout affections are. Health? Weight loss? Control? Christ? Similar to how we discussed prayer, biblical fasting is not a means to get a better body; biblical fasting is a means to get God. Let's remember that.

Coffee Habit

Starbucks is known for being a company that trains its employees well. In his analysis of the company in the book *The Power of Habit*, Charles Duhigg says of their training process, "Starbucks has dozens of routines that employees are taught to use during stressful inflection points."[19] Starbucks knows that unhappy customers are part of the gig, so rather than merely trying to avoid every possible situation in which a customer might be unhappy (which I am sure they do as well), they also train their employees in what to do when that tension occurs. Duhigg says, "This is how willpower becomes a habit: by choosing a certain behavior ahead of time, and then following that routine when the inflection point arrives."

Duhigg isn't purporting faith here, but common grace gives way to wisdom. How you prepare is how you play under pressure. My question for us, friend, is have we done the same? Challenges are part of our lives here. Frustrations in relationships, stress on our finances, health struggles and career difficulties, they are all at some point unavoidable. But the habits we form in turning our hearts to Scripture daily, communicating with the Lord in prayer, and slowly building a store of His Word in our hearts are the routines we want to be able to draw on when those challenges come.

The steadfast love of the Lord never once ceased for Jeremiah. It was always there. But when Jeremiah called it to mind, when he paused to remember it, to direct his mind to it, *then* he had hope. The steadfast love of the Lord has never failed my friends traveling overseas for adoption. It has never failed them in months upon months of paperwork and preparations and waiting. Or on that trip across the world in eight short days. It never failed Darlene Deibler Rose in that Japanese prison camp. But every single one of these people had to call it to mind. They had to fight distraction, fight the urgency of the immediate fear and hopelessness knocking at their hearts. They chose the well-worn path of remembering Him developed though learned habits of knowing Him. Therefore, they have hope. And so can we.

but then she remembered . . . to train well

No matter where you are, think carefully over the past twenty-four hours. **Below, try to list *every* decision you made in those hours. Don't deliberate, just jot them all down.**

Are you sure you got them all? Now, look over those decisions. Put an asterisk by any decision that is a habit for you—something you have done repeatedly and do frequently.

Now circle any decision from your list that took some serious thought or consideration. What is your ratio of decisions by habit to decisions that require more serious thought?

In this chapter we read that more than 99 percent of our daily decisions happen without any immediate reflection, on autopilot almost. Do you find this to be true in your own life? What are the benefits and drawbacks of living on autopilot?

If autopilot is our default, making decisions from the person we have become, our becoming is pretty important. How much thought do you put into the person you are becoming?

Read Romans 8:29. Whose image are we to be conformed to?

Take a look at Romans 12:2. What are we not to conform to?

How are we transformed (also Romans 12:2)?

Are you active about being transformed?

Think through the quarterback analogy from this chapter. What must a quarterback do to prepare? (*Don't get hung up here if sports aren't your thing; no one is grading this assignment. Just use what knowledge you have and make some good guesses if you need to do so.*)
Why do you think we expect preparation in many areas of life but are prone to resist it in our spiritual life?

Read 2 Timothy 4:2. When did Paul say he wanted Timothy to be ready?

Back to verse 1 of that same chapter, Paul is commanding this to Timothy in the presence of whom?

Still in that same chapter, read verses 3 and 4. Why was Paul's command to Timothy both critical and timely?

We don't have to stretch to see a similar time coming in our own world, do we? The Word of God is forever timeless and timely.

Now let's discuss these habits. Be honest: How faithful are you in reading the Bible? How could you, by the smallest sustainable margin, increase your training?

There are many ways to do this right. Begin with the simple goal of faithfulness, of establishing that habit. Once you have formed the habit, there are all sorts of ways to grow with it. You can read through a psalm daily, as my friend Susan has taught me to do. Read through the gospels, join a group reading plan like the Bible Reading Challenge through Christ Church, read chronologically or read the whole Bible in a year. Do an inductive study on one book at a time. Invite a friend for accountability, and grow together. Each of these means can serve you well as long as you are showing up with a heart that seeks to know Christ through His Word. That is a heart He can work with.

Let's talk prayer. How are you growing, currently training, in making your requests known to God?

Read Philippians 4:6–7. Fill in the blanks for the first part of verse 6 below.

Do _____ be _____ about _____

Let's stop there for a second. What exactly are we allowed to be anxious about?

That feels like a clear and hefty instruction, doesn't it? The word for "be anxious" here is a verb, an action, meaning, "to be troubled with cares about." Thankfully Paul does not stop there. He gives us another action instead. **What does the rest of verse 6 tell us?**

This is almost like that excellent Starbucks training we read about. Starbucks has succeeded at training their employees what to do when things get stressful. But guess what, they were just stealing from God's play book. He has prepared us for those worrisome situations. He's saying instead of this, do that. And that is *pray*. **What is the result of this action (v. 7)?**

He doesn't promise that the storm will immediately leave. He promises peace there—a peace beyond what even makes sense, peace that will guard our hearts and our minds in Christ. If we ever needed a reason to develop a reflex of prayer, we've got it here. How do you plan to be active in training?

Memorization. Write down your very first reaction to this idea. Have you always wanted to do it? Does it seem impossible? Do you think you are too old? Or you don't have time for it? Or do you think you are just not good at it? So many of us have disqualified ourselves before we even begin, but here is what I want you to do. Start small. One verse, small. I've listed a couple of great verses below to get started with, but I encourage you to begin a list of your own. The Notes app of your phone can be a great help. Just keep a running list of Scriptures and passages, chapters and books (yes, you can get there!) you would like to memorize and work your way through them.

Is the concept of fasting new to you? What is your experience with fasting?

Read through Jesus's words in Matthew 9:14–15. **When does Jesus say will be the disciples' time of fasting?**

Let's do a little more study. **Read Philippians 3:17–19. The enemies of the cross of Christ, as Paul calls them, who was their god?**

What do they glory in? What are their minds set on?

Now look at Matthew 16:23, Christ's admonition of Peter. **What does Jesus say Peter's mind is set on?**

Fasting is an intentional going without so that we might force ourselves to set our mind on Him. We beg Christ's wisdom, discernment, and holiness to realign our hearts and minds and desires away from the things of this earth and fully toward Him. **How can you train well by practicing fasting?**

Your training honors Him, friend. A heart that follows, that learns, that listens is one the Father can work with. Be patient with yourself as He is patient with you. Be faithful as He is forever faithful. And keep doing the good work of training.

afterword

The world feels noisy and loud, often distracting to a threatening degree. You aren't alone, if you have been feeling that, friend. Technology has certainly changed things, but history has also shown that the world has always been distracting. Francis Schaeffer says, "The central problem is always in the midst of the people of God, not in the circumstances surrounding them."[1] If that reads like a direct hit, remember that God always comes to the aid of His people. He is the God who makes a way, and I am fully convinced that He has already made a way for us to thrive in this loud and distracting world. He has given us means to pay attention to Him, to live with hearts fully oriented toward Him, steadied by the truth of who He is when we remember. We are called to it and created for it. Remember.

The stakes are high in a world that continually positions us to be oriented toward the present moment when we have hearts designed to be set on eternity. There are an ever-increasing number of outlets that would seek to tell us what is important, what to value, what to pay attention to, what to love. But we have the timeless and timely truth of God's Word to guide our hearts and minds here. We must pay attention.

There is a generation rising behind us that needs to know the truth of God's Word. They need to hear our time-worn stories of His faithfulness in our ordinary and every day, of His provision and protection when our world quaked, when tensions were high and there was political unrest. They need to see our stones of remembrance, our slow-growing fruit, our healed scars, so that they will ask about them, and in telling them, we will remember how God has been there and done that, and He will indeed do it again. This is how we sow faith into the hearts of the next generation. God's plan for our remembering is beautiful, friend. He embedded it into creation, into us. Let's be the rememberers. That we might give Him our full attention as we run our race with endurance. To God be the glory.

acknowledgments

These are some of the most precious words to write. For a girl who leans on the strength and dexterity of the written word to communicate powerful and life-giving truth, sometimes those words still seem flimsy and fall short. So I offer them in faith, just as I always do, that a thank-you won't be redundant or trite, that it will be received with the weight of a daughter's heart, who knows she could not ever do this on her own.

Thank you, Jesus, for making a way. Thank you for the opportunity to write, for the strength to do it, and for any bit of knowledge I could possess. You are forever faithful.

Thank you to the entire team at Bethany, who serve with excellence. Thank you, Tawny, for your faithful support. Thank you, Tim, for the life preserver.

Thank you, Curt and Rhonda, Deon, and more friends who offered faithful prayers and cheers and encouragement.

Thank you, Candee and Alesha, Kelly and Lisa—sounding-board friends who are a beautiful part of the storyline of my life.

Thank you, Mom and Dad, for laying good groundwork and never stopping. Still building.

Thank you, Ross, for ever supporting with leadership and strength and vision for the things that really matter. I love building and serving with you. And to Tyler, Bailey, Brooklyn, and Bo: Who knew I would birth the best work, and the best cheerleaders, for this bit of writing I get to do? I thank God for you.

To Him be the glory.

notes

A Note for the Distracted

1. "If anyone loves me, he will keep my word, and my Father will love him, and we will come to him and make our home with him" (John 14:23).

2. Trevor Wheelwright, "2022 Cell Phone Usage Statistics: How Obsessed Are We?" Reviews.org, January 24, 2022, https://www.reviews.org/mobile /cell-phone-addiction/.

3. "For though we walk in the flesh, we are not waging war in the flesh" (2 Corinthians 10:3).

4. Ephesians 6:10–18

5. "Abide in me, and I in you. As the branch cannot bear fruit by itself, unless it abides in the vine, neither can you, unless you abide in me" (John 15:4).

Chapter 1 The World Has Lost Its Memory

1. Consumer Insights, Microsoft Canada, "Attention Spans," Spring 2015, https://dl.motamem.org/microsoft-attention-spans-research-report.pdf.

2. "Attend," American Dictionary of the English Language, https://webstersdictionary1828.com/Dictionary/attend.

3. "Hearken," American Dictionary of the English Language, https://webstersdictionary1828.com/Dictionary/hearken.

4. "Heed," American Dictionary of the English Language, https://webstersdictionary1828.com/Dictionary/heed.

5. "Attention," Merriam-Webster, https://www.merriam-webster.com/dictionary/attention.

6. Carl Trueman, *The Rise and Triumph of the Modern Self* (Wheaton, IL: Crossway, 2020), 30.

7. Mia Jankowicz, "The Coronavirus Outbreak Has Prompted People Around The World To Panic Buy Toilet Paper. Here's Why," Insider, March 10, 2020, https://www.businessinsider.com/coronavirus-panic-buying-toilet -paper-stockpiling-photos-2020-3.

8. Andrew Moore, "How the Coronavirus Created a Toilet Paper Shortage," NC State—College of Natural Resources, May 19, 2020, https://cnr.ncsu.edu /news/2020/05/coronavirus-toilet-paper-shortage/.

9. Exodus 14:11

10. Exodus 16:3

11. Exodus 17:3

12. See Exodus 10:2; 12:17; 12:26; 13:14; 16:32.

13. Psalm 106:7–8

14. Psalm 106:1

15. Marvin M. Chun and Nicholas B. Turk-Browne, "Interactions between Attention and Memory," Science Direct, March 2007, https://ntblab.yale.edu /wp-content/uploads/2015/01/Chun_CONB_2007.pdf.

16. "Set your minds on things that are above, not on things that are on earth" (Colossians 3:2).

17. "His divine power has granted to us all things that pertain to life and godliness" (2 Peter 1:3).

18. Matthew Henry: Commentary on Philippians 3, https://www.blueletter bible.org/Comm/mhc/Phl/Phl_003.cfm?a=1106013.

19. Matthew Henry: Commentary on Philippians 3.

Chapter 2 Beginning with What We Must Know

1. A. W. Tozer, *The Knowledge of the Holy* (New York: HarperCollins, 1978), 1.

2. Philippians 3:1

3. Philippians 3:8

4. Philippians 3:8, 10

5. Colossians 3:10

6. Romans 11:33 CSB

7. Isaiah 40:13, 14, 28

8. Deuteronomy 6:2

9. Tim Mackie, "What Is the Shema Prayer?" Bible Project, 2017, https:// bibleproject.com/blog/what-is-the-shema/.

10. Deuteronomy 6:6 NLT

11. Deuteronomy 6:12

12. Rick Hellman, "Study Reveals How We Spend Our Time during a Social Media Fast," University of Kansas, November 9, 2018, https://today.ku.edu /2018/11/09/abstention-reveals-what-social-media-displaces.

13. Dr. Margie Warrell, "Combatting Attention Distraction Disorder: The Ultimate Tool," Forbes, November 28, 2012, https://www.forbes.com /sites/margiewarrell/2012/11/28/combatting-attention-distraction-disorder /?sh=6693db895035.

14. Ally Mintzer, "Paying Attention: The Attention Economy," *Berkeley Economic Review*, March 31, 2020, https://econreview.berkeley.edu/paying-attention-the-attention-economy/.

15. Barbara Hughes, *Disciplines of a Godly Woman* (Wheaton, IL: Crossway, 2001), 45.

16. John 3:16 as quoted in *Disciplines of a Godly Woman*, 28.

17. Matthew 16:15–16

18. Matthew Henry, Commentary on Psalm 139, https://www.blueletterbible.org/Comm/mhc/Psa/Psa_139.cfm?a=617014.

19. Mintzer, "Paying Attention."

20. Psalm 139:14

Chapter 3 Actions that Bring Us Back to Remembrance

1. "I think it right, as long as I am in this body, to stir you up by way of reminder" (2 Peter 1:13).

2. Genesis 7:23

3. Genesis 7:11 NLT

4. Isaiah 49:15 NLT

5. Genesis 40:14

6. Exodus 14:10

7. "Israel saw the great power that the Lord used against the Egyptians, so the people feared the Lord, and they believed in the Lord and in his servant Moses" (Exodus 14:31).

8. You have read *We're Going on a Bear Hunt*, haven't you?

9. Joshua 1:16–17

10. Joshua 4:3

11. Joshua 4:21–22

12. "Memorial Stones," Ligonier.org, January 10, 2019, https://www.ligonier.org/learn/devotionals/memorial-stones.

13. Joshua 4:23-24

14. Wayne Grudem, *Systematic Theology* (Leicester, England: InterVarsity Press, 1994), 989.

15. Revelation 19:6–7

16. Revelation 19:9

17. Exodus 12:14, 17

18. Luke 22:15

19. Dr. Sinclair B. Ferguson, "The First and Last Supper," Blue Letter Bible, www.blueletterbible.org/audio_video/popPlayer.cfm?type=sa&id=72712125023&rel=SermonAudio/Ferguson,%20Sinclair%20B.

20. Ferguson, "The First and Last Supper."

21. 1 Corinthians 11:23–25

22. Grudem, *Systematic Theology*, 990.

23. Matthew Henry, Commentary on Luke 22, https://www.blueletterbible.org/Comm/mhc/Luk/Luk_022.cfm?a=995019.

24. "For whatever was written in former days was written for our instruction, that through endurance and through the encouragement of the Scriptures we might have hope" (Romans 15:4).

25. Grudem, *Systematic Theology*, 980–981.

26. Grudem, *Systematic Theology*, 981.

27. Acts 2:38

28. Matthew 28:18–19

29. Galatians 3:27

30. Kendra Cherry, "A Simple DIY Short-Term Memory Experiment," VerywellMIND, May 3, 2020, https://www.verywellmind.com/a-short-term-memory-experiment-2795664.

Chapter 4 Who You Are and How You Were Made

1. Come on, name that movie. . . . *The Sound of Music*!

2. "Identity," APA Dictionary of Psychology, https://dictionary.apa.org/identity.

3. James D. Fearon, "What Is Identity (as We Now Use the Word)?" abstract (Stanford University, 1999), 2, https://web.stanford.edu/group/fearon-research/cgi-bin/wordpress/wp-content/uploads/2013/10/What-is-Identity-as-we-now-use-the-word-.pdf.

4. Philip Gleason, "Identifying Identity: A Semantic History," *The Journal of American History* 69, vol. 4, March 1, 1983): 910, https://doi.org/10.2307/1901196.

5. Melonyce McAfee, "'Identity' Is the Dictionary.com 2015 Word of the Year," CNN, December 8, 2015, https://www.cnn.com/2015/12/08/living/word-of-the-year-dictionary-com-feat/index.html.

6. Proverbs 1:7

7. Nahum 1:5, 7

8. "Every good gift and every perfect gift is from above, coming down from the Father of lights, with whom there is no variation or shadow due to change" (James 1:17).

9. Michael Wesch, *The Art of Being Human* (Kansas State University: New Prarie Press 2018), 112.

10. Wesch, *The Art of Being Human*, 113.

11. Wesch, *The Art of Being Human*, 113.

12. "Whatever you do, work heartily, as for the Lord and not for men" (Colossians 3:23).

13. James 1:17 NLT

14. Joshua Pauling, "Keep Finding Your Identity in Christ," *American Reformer*, March 31, 2022, https://americanreformer.org/2022/03/keep-finding-your-identity-in-christ/.

Chapter 5 God's View of Time, Not Ours

1. Paul Tripp, "Idolatry of the Body," Wednesday Word, September 15, 2021, https://www.paultripp.com/wednesdays-word/posts/idolatry-of-the-body.

2. John 4:23

3. "But when the fullness of time had come, God sent forth his Son, born of woman, born under the law" (Galatians 4:4).

4. John 2:3-4

5. Matthew 26: 40–41

6. Matthew 26:45

7. John 4:32, 34

8. Matthew 6:25–27

9. "So teach us to number our days that we may get a heart of wisdom" (Psalm 90:12).

10. Chip Heath and Dan Heath, *Made to Stick* (New York: Random House, 2007), 25.

11. Heath and Heath, *Made to Stick*, 26.

12. Luke 10:25–37

13. Matthew Henry, Commentary on Ecclesiastes 3, https://www.blueletter bible.org/Comm/mhc/Ecc/Ecc_003.cfm?a=662001.

14. Luke 2:49 NKJV

Chapter 6 Say So

1. See Acts 9, Acts 22, and Acts 26.

2. Philippians 3:1

3. 2 Peter 1:13

4. Jude 5

5. G. K. Chesterton, *Orthodoxy* (Chicago: Moody Publishers, 2009), 98.

6. "Monotony," Online Etymology Dictionary, https://www.etymonline .com/word/monotony.

7. Matthew Henry, Commentary on Psalm 96, https://www.blueletterbible .org/Comm/mhc/Psa/Psa_096.cfm?a=574002.

8. Rod Dreher, *Live Not by Lies* (New York: Sentinel, 2020), 127.

9. Jeffrey Karpicke PhD, "A Powerful Way to Improve Learning and Memory," Psychological Science Agenda, June 2016, https://www.apa.org/science /about/psa/2016/06/learning-memory.

10. "So teach us to number our days that we may get a heart of wisdom" (Psalm 90:12).

11. W. E. Vine, *Vine's Complete Expository Dictionary* (Nashville: Thomas Nelson), 125.

12. Henry, Commentary on Psalm 96.

Chapter 7 Remembering When You Feel Weak

1. Paul David Tripp, *Awe* (Wheaton, IL: Crossway, 2015), 65.
2. 2 Kings 6:12
3. 2 Kings 6:15 CSB
4. 2 Kings 6:16–17
5. "He knows our frame; he remembers that we are dust" (Psalm 103:14).
6. John 14:26
7. Endel Tulving and Fergus I. M. Craik, eds., *The Oxford Handbook of Memory* (New York: Oxford University Press, 2000), 27.
8. Lawrence Patihis, Steven J. Frenda, Aurora K. R. LePort, et al., "False Memories in Highly Superior Autobiographical Memory Individuals," Proceedings of the National Academy of Sciences, November 18, 2013, https://www.pnas.org/doi/full/10.1073/pnas.1314373110.
9. Deuteronomy 6:5–9, 12
10. Deuteronomy 6:20–25
11. Luke 22:19
12. Deuteronomy 6:21–24
13. Deuteronomy 6:24
14. Deuteronomy 6:25
15. "The fear of the LORD is hatred of evil" (Proverbs 8:13).
16. "Submit yourselves therefore to God. Resist the devil, and he will flee from you" (James 4:7).
17. "If you do not do well, sin is crouching at the door. Its desire is contrary to you, but you must rule over it" (Genesis 4:7).
18. John 13:1 NLT
19. Matthew Henry, https://www.blueletterbible.org/Comm/mhc/Jhn/Jhn_013.cfm?a=1010001
20. John 13:21
21. Matthew 26:22
22. 2 Corinthians 12:9
23. 2 Corinthians 12:9–10
24. John 20:26–27
25. Matthew 11:28

Chapter 8 Habit Forming

1. David Mathis, *Habits of Grace* (Wheaton, IL: Crossway, 2016), 63.
2. Ephesians 4:1
3. Romans 12:1–2
4. Matthew Henry, Commentary on Romans 12, https://www.blueletterbible.org/Comm/mhc/Rom/Rom_012.cfm.
5. "If my people who are called by my name humble themselves, and pray and seek my face and turn from their wicked ways, then I will hear from heaven and will forgive their sin and heal their land" (2 Chronicles 7:14).
6. 1 Corinthians 9:25–27

7. "For the things that are seen are transient, but the things that are unseen are eternal" (2 Corinthians 4:18).

8. "Do not be deceived: God is not mocked, for whatever one sows, that will he also reap" (Galatians 6:7).

9. Jeremiah 2:6–7

10. Lamentations 3:19–20

11. Lamentations 3:21–24

12. John Mark Comer, *The Ruthless Elimination of Hurry* (New York: WaterBrook, 2019), 134.

13. "Christians Don't Read Their Bible," Ponce Foundation, n.d., http://ponce foundation.com/christians-dont-read-their-bible/.

14. Oswald Chambers, *If You Will Ask* (Grand Rapids, MI: Discovery House Publishers, 1994), 10.

15. David Mathis, *Habits of Grace*, 94.

16. Why Memorizing Things (Though a Lost Art) Isn't a Waste of Time," HealthEssentials, September 11, 2018. https://health.clevelandclinic.org/why -memorizing-things-though-a-lost-art-isnt-a-waste-of-time/.

17. Darlene Deibler Rose, *Evidence Not Seen* (Harper: SanFrancisco, 1990), 143.

18. *Matthew Henry Commentary of the Whole Bible* quoted in Whitney, *Spiritual Disciplines for the Christian Life*, 214.

19. Charles Duhigg, *The Power of Habit* (Random House, New York: 2012), 146.

Afterword

1. Francis Schaeffer, *The Lord's Work in the Lord's Way* (Wheaton, IL, Crossway), 10.

about the author

Katie Westenberg is first a follower of Christ, a wife, and a mom growing faithfully alongside her four children. She believes boldly in the transformative power of faith in Jesus Christ. As an author and speaker, she teaches women to grow a robust theology of who God is, become students of Scripture, and learn to live out that truth with courage. She serves a thriving community of women at www.katiewestenberg.com, and makes her home in the lovely Pacific Northwest.

MORE FROM
KATIE WESTENBERG

Digging deep into Scripture, Katie Westenberg shows that finding the courage to overcome our fears starts with fear of the Lord. In this book, you will discover a fresh take on an old truth to displace fear, find practical direction on how to overcome fear, and access the holy courage you were made for—resulting in tremendous freedom!

I Choose Brave